ways to help them learn

early childhood · birth to 5yrs.

G/L REGAL BOOKS™

INTERNATIONAL CENTER FOR LEARNING

A Division of G/L Publications, Glendale, California, U.S.A.

Second printing, 1972
Third printing, 1973
Fourth printing, 1974
Fifth printing, 1974

Published by Regal Books Division, G/L Publications, Glendale, California 91209, U.S.A.
Library of Congress Catalog Card No. 73-168842. ISBN 0-8307-0118-4

Photo Credits: Page *viii*, 38, 88, 118: David J. Pavol. Page 16: Bryan McClelland. Page 28, 126: Dick Reynolds. Page 48: Bruce Benton. Page 60,72,80,96,136: Alan Cliburn.

CONTENTS

NOTE: For detailed information on ways to organize Early Childhood Departments and to equip these facilities, read *Ways to Plan and Organize Your Sunday School: Early Childhood.*

THE AUTHOR

Dolores Rowen graduated from the University of Redlands with a B.A. degree in education. She is currently studying in the field of Early Childhood Education at the University of California at Los Angeles. Her teaching career began in New Jersey, and she now teaches kindergarten in the Los Angeles Unified School District.

Dolores has traveled extensively throughout the United States, Europe, the Holy Land, the South Pacific, Australia and Asia. She spent her sabbatical leave studying schools for deaf children in Australia.

Active at Bel Air Presbyterian Church, Dolores is presently Coordinator of the Early Childhood Division of the Sunday school. She is also an experienced workshop leader and free-lance writer for G/L Publications, focusing her attention on Early Childhood curricula.

FOREWORD

The late Dr. Henrietta C. Mears, founder of Gospel Light Publications and distinguished Christian education leader for more than 40 years, often said, "Good teachers are not born; they are made by conscientious labor." It is axiomatic that if one is to be successful in any field, he must be trained. Our Lord recognized this fact in training the Twelve. First He spent the whole night in prayer in preparation for the momentous task of choosing them. From this point the teaching and training of these men became a matter of paramount importance to Him.

A tremendous passion for the training of leadership has been a hallmark in the program of Gospel Light. What workers learn today will determine what the church will be tomorrow. This is the great need of the hour; to train leaders for Christian service, and particularly the Sunday school, people who will know how to administer and teach. With a deep sense of obligation as well as opportunity the International Center for Learning was created in 1970 to specialize in the training of dedicated personnel in all departments of the local church.

This is one of a series of textbooks designed to train workers in the Sunday school. It has grown out of actual proven experience and represents the best educational philosophy. In addition to textual materials, the full program of ICL includes audio visual media and church leadership training seminars sponsored in strategic centers across America and ultimately overseas as rapidly as God enables. We are being deluged with requests to help in the momentous task of training workers. We dare not stop short of providing all possible assistance.

Train for Sunday school success! Train for church growth! Train people by example and experience to pray and plan and perform. Christ trained the Twelve. Dare we do less?

President, Gospel Light Publications

A WORD OF EXPLANATION

As three stonemasons were working, each one was asked, "What are you doing?"

"Laying stone," was the first reply.

"Making a wall," the second man answered.

"Building a cathedral," the third stonemason said.

As three Sunday school teachers were moving about from child to child, each one was asked, "What are you doing?"

"Baby sitting these kids," the first teacher answered.

"Caring for children," the second replied.

"Sharing God's love," the third teacher said.

How does one go about sharing the gospel of God's love with little ones? What can this message of redemption and reconciliation possibly mean to a young child?

Many of the basic and vital truths from God's Word can be made relevant to a young child when they are expressed in ways within his understanding. He learns about his world and the people in it through firsthand experiences—seeing, touching, doing, hearing, smelling, tasting. When it is expressed in these terms, God's love can then become real and meaningful to a young child.

You, the person God has chosen to express His love, are a vital factor in making that love a reality in the child's life. As a member of God's family of believers, you have experienced God's love, concern, dependability and forgiveness. So, because of your relationship with the Lord, you are equipped to express these concepts to the child. Then he in turn begins to feel some of God's unconditional and everpresent love.

Part I of this book has been prepared to help you become acquainted with young children, their general pattern of growth and development; their possible responses to specific situations. This section also states Bible teaching objectives in terms of a child's learning level.

Part II defines learning as it applies to Bible truths; also the teacher's role in helping a child to learn effectively in a Sunday morning setting.

Part III offers a variety of ways to help a child learn Bible truths—method and material suggestions that make learning a pleasant and rewarding experience for both child and teacher.

Guiding young children is an awesome task, you say? Yes, indeed! No other task on earth is of more consequence than that of helping young children learn basic, vital scriptural truth. However, God has not left you alone to accomplish this task in your own strength. He offers you the instruction of the Holy Spirit and the promise of His guidance.

If you want to know what God wants you to do, ask Him and He will gladly tell you, for He is always ready to give a bountiful supply of wisdom to all who ask Him; He will not resent it. But when you ask Him, be sure that you really expect Him to tell you, for a doubtful mind will be as un-settled as a wave of the sea that is driven and tossed by the wind; and every decision you then make will be uncertain, as you turn first this way, and then that. If you don't ask with faith, don't expect the Lord to give you any solid answer. (James 1:5-8 *The Living Bible.*)

PART I

THE LEARNER

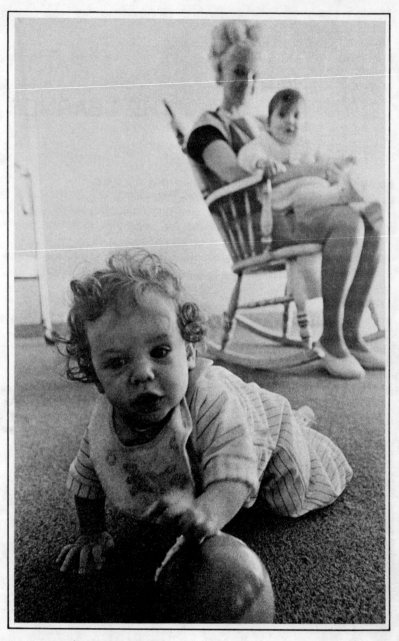

CHAPTER ONE

BIRTH TO TWO

Every child is a unique miracle of God's making. From the time of his birth each one is different from all others. God planned it so. No one individual will react or grow in quite the same way as another. Individual differences are readily apparent in even the youngest babies. Although all are different, nevertheless little ones have needs that are much the same. Each child passes through essentially the same growth pattern, but at his own rate of speed. Being aware of these stages of development helps those who work with little ones better understand ways to guide them.

AT THE BEGINNING OF HIS LIFE, A BABY LEARNS ABOUT HIS WORLD THROUGH PEOPLE.

When they adequately and consistently meet his needs, he learns love and trust. He feels security in the firm, gentle hands and arms that hold him. Out of this kind of love he learns he is cared for and his needs are regularly satisfied. This love and trust is the foundation upon which a child can build his personal response to God and to His love.

AS THE INFANT GROWS AND DEVELOPS, HE GRADUALLY RESPONDS TO HIS ENVIRONMENT.

He laughs, smiles, cries, accepts and rejects. The way in which his needs are met now determines in large part the way his personality develops later. For instance, exchanging smiles with a nursery worker is the infant's first lesson in love. Gently approach the baby by making soft, soothing sounds. Hold him, reassure him and make him comfortable in a safe, warm environment. Consistently reflect God's love and gladness as you feed, clothe and change him. Then he will expect what he has come to know.

Sing-song rhymes and simple songs are a natural kind of conversation with babies. Singing and humming provide soothing kinds of sounds that contribute to a peaceful atmosphere. Babies soon begin to respond to favorites such as "Jesus Loves Children"[1] and "By, Low My Baby",[1] when they are sung or hummed again and again.

Your calm, gentle tone of voice helps babies to feel reassured long before they understand your words. Avoid baby talk. Use short simple sentences with words that mean exactly what they say. "God loves Tommy. I love Tommy," said with a smile helps Tommy begin to associate the word "God" with a pleasant experience.

"The place is here; the time is now; the person is ME," is a baby's view of his world. When he feels a need, he wants it satisfied—now! Almost every baby finds it unbearable to have to wait to be fed and cries loudly when hungry. But as he grows physically, his need is not so immediate and he learns to trust adults to meet his need without the demanding.

AS A BABY'S FIRST MONTHS PASS, HIS SOCIAL AWARENESS BEGINS TO INCREASE.

He knows his regular nursery worker and recognizes the friendly touch of loving hands supporting him and cuddling him. How important then, that a staff of regular workers be maintained so that little ones can begin to build an identity with his "friend at church."

AT ABOUT SIX MONTHS THE INFANT OFTEN QUITE SUDDENLY BECOMES SHY AND AFRAID OF STRANGERS.

At this point he begins to see himself as a separate person. As a newborn, he could not separate his own body from the rest of the world. Now he slowly begins to learn about himself as an individual. When a baby expresses his fears in crying and screaming, try approaching him with a quiet smile and reassuring words. He'll probably respond to your gentle concern. He may even give you a smile in return! Your expressions of love are contagious. The result may be twofold. First, you will be in a mood to deal patiently and kindly with the baby's problem. And second, the baby will probably relax and begin to feel less tense. Avoid reflecting the baby's mood. When a child displays anger, the worker often feels a bit angry, too. A gentle, calm worker will generally have a quieting effect on the baby.

DURING THE CHILD'S SECOND HALF YEAR, CHANGES COME ALMOST FASTER THAN WE CAN CHART THEM.

His ability to move around improves almost daily. He crawls actively and sits upright for a period of time. The first teeth begin to come in and solid food is added to his diet. The creeper explores the world with his mouth—biting and tasting everything within his grasp. He grabs a toy, puts it in his mouth, takes it out, changes hands, bangs the toy on the crib, drops it, bangs his fist in protest, cries and then repeats the sequence all over again. After he learns to pinch his thumb and forefinger together, he tries to hold his bottle and feed himself.

The creeper pulls himself up on furniture and stands alone. He exerts his independence by crawling away, resisting dressing, refusing a bottle, kicking and screaming. As the child nears his first birthday, he walks holding onto furniture and takes his first independent step. The age for walking depends on the child's temperament, general body build, cautiousness, courage, food and exercise.

Once a child has left his crib for crawling or walking experiences, safety measures are of vital consideration. Check equipment for sharp edges, loose pieces, cleanliness, chipping paint or any other potential safety hazard. Also check doors, windows or any openings through which a child might venture.

THE CHILD APPROACHING ONE YEAR ENJOYS SIMPLE GAMES AND SIMPLE SONGS.

He begins to imitate sounds and learns to distinguish

the tone of voice of people around him. He plays hide and seek but wants to be found quickly. He responds happily to surprises and wants to be included in the activities of the people around him. Either before or after his first birthday he says his first word.

FACILITIES FOR BABY CARE AT CHURCH MUST TAKE INTO CONSIDERATION ALL OF THE YOUNG CHILD'S NEEDS.

Infants and babies up to the toddler stage need a room of their own with equipment designed for their age. Existing facilities, time and money will determine the modifications you decide to make.

The room in your church used for crib care needs to be well lighted, adequately ventilated and heated. It should also be close to ground floor exits. Equipment needed in the room: room identification signs, reception desk to receive babies, an identification tag for each baby (noneatable) to be pinned to back of clothing with a safety pin, labels for belongings, toilet facilities, safe, sturdy, space-saving cribs, rocking chair, enamel carts or built-in changing tables, wall clock, electric bottle warmers, a sink or other water supply, playpens and storage for diaper bags on shelving or in cabinets out of the child's reach. Clean sheets for each crib each week are a must; also soled soft slippers for the leaders to wear in the room. (High heels are dangerous with creeping babies.) If your workers wear smocks, these must be washed before each wearing. The floor of the room should be thoroughly cleaned each week. Warm crib covers, extra or disposable diapers and wastebaskets are also necessary equipment. On the changing table or on shelves out of the child's reach keep supplies of washcloths or sponges, terry and paper towels, tissues, plastic bags and wax paper, cotton balls, baby oil, lotion, powder and extra safety pins. Use plastic or paper containers rather than glass. Place baby on a square of wax paper to change him and then wrap the diaper in the wax paper or in a plastic bag. Show the child you are glad to do this for him to make him comfortable. Young children are quick to sense any displeasure you have in changing his diaper.

Ask parents for baby's feeding schedule in writing. Then follow it exactly. Feed, burp and rock baby without rushing. Humming and soft singing help him back to sleep.

A record player and records or a small cassette player provide soft background music.

For older babies and creepers who want to move about, provide warm and clean floor space. Small playpens of lightweight, easy-to-clean nylon, jumper chairs and low chairs with attached tables are desirable pieces of equipment to have for the creeper. Toys include washable fabric books, washable toys and cardboard backed pictures covered with transparent plastic for little fingers to touch.

Toys, bed rails and playpen rails need to be sterilized after each use. Keep a solution of Zephiran chloride (available from your druggist) in a safe place in the room. Use two tablespoons of Zephiran chloride concentrate with one gallon of water or use equal amounts of Zephiran chloride aqueous and water. Place wet toys on a towel to dry.

Advertise on your parents' bulletin board (in outside hall) and in your church bulletin that you have a "well baby" nursery. Tactfully ask parents with sick children to care for them at home where they will get well faster and not infect other babies. Workers also must always be in good health while caring for the children. Check with the health department in your city or county for requirements and standards for child care facilities, supervision and space.

STOP! Before continuing, think about the crib care facilities in your church in terms of what you've read in this chapter:

- ☐ *Are the nursery workers in good health, regular in attendance?*
- ☐ *Do they express love and kindness to the little ones in their care?*
- ☐ *Are the facilities cleaned after each use? Bedding changed? Toys sterilized? Floor scrubbed?*

TODDLERS

Walking brings many changes to the child and everyone around him. From now on life is a compromise between the toddler's fierce desire to manage everything and the adult's good sense about what his behavior shows he needs. Routines and activities both at church and at home must be kept simple for a growing child with lots of interests and no sense of danger. His environment must be safe for his explorings.

BASIC TO A CHILD'S WELFARE IS HIS NEED TO FEEL LOVED AND ACCEPTED BY THE ADULTS IN HIS LIFE.

He must feel love and acceptance even when the things he does are unacceptable. Help him know that you still love him, even though you must redirect his behavior. When he is behaving well, give lots of praise as you identify his acceptable actions. "Just look how still Jeff stands while I wash his face!"

At each new step in his development, workers need to help the toddler learn basic acceptable behavior. Distracting him with a toy, conversation or activity can prevent stubborn resistance. Adults who are consistently firm and friendly, yet understanding of individual differences, help the child learn to control his impulses and develop his own self-control.

The relationship of the child to his nursery worker is of greater importance than his schedule or activities. The toddler who has learned to love and trust the adults in his life is able to confidently explore his surroundings and experience new feelings and new elements in his life. He learns through the affection, patience, and understanding the adults in his life display toward him.

A TODDLER HAS A TREMENDOUS URGE TO BE INDEPENDENT.

He walks, climbs, falls, undresses himself, feeds himself and invades the activities of other children. His view of the world is directly related to his growing ability to use his body. No matter how hard he tries and you encourage him, he cannot exercise much deliberate control over his own behavior. He needs space in which to move around in and to practice movements which gradually become more relaxed and more refined.

A toddler is concerned mostly about himself. An expanding range of emotions, social relationships and reactions to his environment become apparent. He treats other children the same as objects. He pokes a finger in an ear and tastes an arm with the same curiosity as he approaches a new toy. He likes to be near other children but he does not know how to play with others. He lacks the maturity to share toys and he should not be forced to do so. Duplicates of favorite toys allow several children to play without the frustrations of having to take turns. The one year old has no sense of what will come in the future, no sense of planning ahead. Now is what is important.

TO A TODDLER PHYSICAL PLAY, EVEN GENTLY ROUGHHOUSING ON THE FLOOR, IS ENDLESSLY SATISFYING.

He loves to be noisily followed—and caught! He has boundless energy and ideas for play. Playtime helps him develop self-reliance, knowledge of his own powers and confidence in his own abilities. The delightful cooing infant of a year ago becomes a bossy, self-oriented toddler in constant motion.

Puzzle toys such as nesting cans or cups, strings of snap beads, shaped toys which fit over spindles or into containers encourage the child to practice coordinating his muscles and his eyes. A varied selection of toys gives each child the opportunity to play at his present level and to move on to a toy offering more challenge when he is ready.

THE GROWING CHILD BEGINS TO EXPERIENCE DELIGHT, ELATION, DISTRESS, FEAR AND DISPLEASURE.

He is aware of the feelings of others around him and is sensitive to their expressions of anxiety. He has a great desire to be loved and wants to show his affection in return. He often imitates the actions of adults and tries hard to be what he believes they expect of him.

THE TODDLER NEEDS HELP FROM ADULTS, EVEN THOUGH HE TRIES TO RUN HIS LIFE WITHOUT THEM.

He reaches for door knobs and marches up steps while exercising his capacity to be a separate person. As an infant he thought his mother was part of himself —the part that got things done. Now he discovers he can do things himself and this is at the same time exciting and frightening. Bold, independent action is followed by a rush to the familiar security of the nursery worker or mother. The strong desire for his mother shows that the job of loving and caring for him has been well done.

In this see-saw world, the toddler inexpertly pushes to grow faster and falls back on the love and support of people he trusts. His drive for independence builds on the feelings of safety and love established as an infant. This active trust and sense of security frees the child to begin to know Jesus as someone who loves and cares for him. Without a real and physical sense of trust, the young child could have difficulty understanding God's love and provision for him.

A TODDLER TESTS LIMITS AS HE DEMANDS HIS OWN WAY.

He often refuses the commands of adults he loves. He is battling for independence and selfhood. Leaders at church and parents at home must decide between those things the child can do alone and the things which have to be restricted for the child's safety. The freedom to explore, test and try things out gives the child the feeling that life is something he can handle. Leaders need to respond to the child by listening attentively, expressing interest in what interests him; by being fair in guiding and correcting the child.

YOUNG CHILDREN DO NOT WAIT FOR FORMAL TEACHING SITUATIONS BEFORE THEY LEARN.

From the moment of birth, they learn from the attitudes and actions of those around them. One of the nursery worker's greatest opportunities to help a child is to capitalize on this learning potential. Little ones need to see, touch, smell, hear and taste to learn about their world and the people in it. Nature materials which the child can touch help him accept as real your statements that, "God made this smooth rock . . . pretty flower, etc." Let children hear a seashell, feel lamb's wool, taste a graham cracker, smell a pine cone and see brightly colored pictures.

Brief, simple stories and conversations help a child build an interest in God. Pictures of the world he knows help the child learn more about things he has experienced. These include pictures of parents, church, nature, animals. Talk with him about the pictures. Use short simple sentences. Say, "Here is a bird. God made the bird," as you point to the pictured bird. Frequent story conversations which include his name help the toddler grow in his awareness of God and God's love for him. Repetition of stories reinforces these concepts and ideas.

Imaginative play begins after the child is a year and a half. He expresses himself, copies gestures and voice inflections, releases anger and frustration, relives experiences which are enjoyable or upsetting. A toddler is attracted to a doll he can hold, cuddle, rock and talk to as the worker talks with him. A child can express to a doll experiences he has with other people in his life. He can use the doll as an outlet to be a mother, father, brother or sister. When he comes and brings the doll to you, he means, "Let's be friends. Come play with me."

Singing, chanting and impromptu storytelling using the child's name bring whole-hearted response from the child. He responds to rhythm and made-up songs about the play activity. You can change the words of a song the child knows (see "Clapping"¹) to fit the activity you are doing together. The fun you have together is far more important than the quality of your music or composition!

Sometimes play requires only the child's own arms and legs and room to move. At other times he may involve blocks, empty cartons, chairs, blankets and toys as part of his experience. Large hollow blocks allow toddlers to practice inventiveness. Rocking chairs, baby buggies and play telephones offer endless opportunities for the exploring child.

PLAY HAS A DEFINITE PURPOSE FOR THE CHILD.

This is his job—to learn by doing and imitation. The toddler is interested at different times in dolls, stuffed animals, push-and-pull toys, trucks, cars, lawn mowers, wagons, carpet sweepers, trains, balls and a doll bed—all child-sized, durable and washable. All toys must be evaluated according to safety, age level appropriateness and quality of construction.

LANGUAGE GRADUALLY BECOMES MORE IMPORTANT TO THE TODDLER WITH EACH PASSING MONTH.

For awhile he uses a single word to express a complete thought. "Water," means, "I'm thirsty. May I have a drink?" As the child begins to talk, he also begins to retain what is spoken to him. Nursery workers can tell the child specific information which he can remember as words and not just feelings. Opportunities for beginning prayer are natural now. There are "pretty flowers," "milk and cookies," "mommy and daddy," "our church" or "my friends" for which to thank God. Brief Bible Thoughts such as, *God cares about you,*[2] and *God made everything,*[3] *may* be used very simply in conversation and repeated over and over on a weekly basis. Praying aloud even before the child can talk and join you tells him praying is important to you; and he will want to pray as soon as he is able to talk.

THE CHILD APPROACHING TWO CONTINUES TO PUSH OUT, FINDING HIMSELF AS A SEPARATE PERSON.

He can now run away from a worker, scream in defiance, make people unhappy, climb on furniture, jump off steps or decide to cooperate in a most charming and disarming way. No matter how exasperating he may be, the toddler needs love, patience, kindness and time. He is neither reasonable nor dependable. He is still exploring, deciding and learning what the world is and who he is.

A toddler nearing his second birthday can begin to recognize the rights of others and make choices with other people in mind. When the child feels at ease and happy he will be more cooperative. He needs self-dignity and self-respect in order to have appreciation and esteem for others. With loving guidance and supervision, toddlers can play along side each other although the desire to share and play with others does not come until later. The young child can begin to help put toys away on storage shelves. He can't do the job himself. As you help him, take time for a friendly talk and an opportunity to give the child individual attention. If he decides not to help or not to come along when you call, continue the activity. The child's natural drive to be active will probably pull him into whatever you are doing regardless of his spoken "no." Try whispering a suggestion to a child. He may whisper back, enchanted with the air of mystery and scarcely able to contain himself until beginning your new idea.

As the child nears two years old, his appetite declines. His muscle control develops to the point where his body is ready and he is interested in toilet training. This is another important step towards independence. In a nearby rest room, have a child-size toilet and washbowl for each 8 to 10 toddlers.

PREPARE TODDLERS FOR THEIR PROMOTION INTO THE TWO YEAR OLD SUNDAY SCHOOL DEPARTMENT.

As he approaches the age of two (or two years, three or six months) when he will move on to another department, arrange an advance visit. Talk with him enthusiastically about what he can do in the new department; that he has now grown big enough to do these things. Encourage his parents to recognize the capabilities of their child and the importance of regular Sunday school attendance in his growing and learning years.

IN PREPARING A ROOM FOR TODDLERS, SEPARATE THEM COMPLETELY FROM THE BABIES AND CREEPERS EITHER BY SUBSTANTIAL ROOM DIVIDERS OR WALLS WITH DOORS THAT CLOSE.

The room should be adequately heated and ventilated, well lighted with low windows. The room also needs a rest room nearby. A first floor location close to an exit is a good safety factor in case of fire. Approximately 30 to 35 square feet per child is desirable as is lots of storage space. A linoleum or vinyl tile floor must be thoroughly cleaned each week. In the room you need: a wall clock, a few cribs, playpens, an adult rocking chair, child-size tables and chairs and a water supply. Include a variety of washable toys. Room dividers can be shelves and cupboards or bookcases for toy storage. The cribs need clean sheets for each use and lightweight blankets. You will need to keep on hand disposable diapers, extra panties, paper cups, tissues, plastic bibs, electric bottle warmers, wax paper, washcloths and soap, towels, Band-aids and antiseptic. A bulletin board on the wall outside the door to the room allows you to arrange welcoming seasonal decorations and post messages for parents.

Additional items to include in the toddler's environment are a goldfish tank, plants, flowers, turtles, an ant farm under glass and a seashell. A record player and records or cassette player provides continuous background music with minimum attention from leaders. Have a large, sturdy Bible with colorful pictures and allow children to touch it. (The Bible at home is probably off limits to the inquisitive child.) Let him touch it as you tell him, "The Bible is a special book, Tim. It tells us God loves each one of us. God loves you, Tim."

THE TODDLER ENJOYS EXPLORING HIS SURROUNDINGS BY POKING HIS FINGERS INTO HOLES AND CORNERS WITHOUT REGARD TO HIS OWN SAFETY OR THE COMFORT OF ANOTHER PERSON.

He is fascinated by things to touch, punch, handle, smell, bite and squeeze. Climbing, pushing, pulling contribute to the development of the child's large muscles. Coordination of finer muscles develops through manipulating toys that the child can lift, drag, stack and dump. He likes simple, brightly colored pictures in books with large cardboard pages he can turn himself. Plastic, linen and cloth are appropriate pages for baby books. The toddler can see and touch the pages. He can pull the book around and chew on a corner. During a story he needs to see the picture in the book as the nursery worker holds it open.

STOP! *Before continuing, evaluate the toddler room of your church:*

- ☐ *Is the room clean—really clean—and well ventilated?*
- ☐ *Is there enough open floor space (35 square feet per child) for toddlers to move about?*
- ☐ *Is there one worker for each five children?*
- ☐ *Are there toys to encourage large muscle activity, such as a rocking boat?*
- ☐ *Is all equipment absolutely safe?*

CHAPTER TWO

THE TWO YEAR OLD

For everything there is an appointed season, and there is a proper time for every project under heaven.[1]

At the right time—God's time—a child is born and his own unique personality begins to unfold. The miracle of growth begins. Each child grows and develops as an individual; he is different from all others. During these years of early childhood he will grow faster and learn more than at any other period in his life.

The qualities that come with being young are not imperfections or flaws. Early childhood is not a disease to be endured or cured—like measles or a cold! Rather, early childhood is a marked and definable stage in development with certain basic tasks to be achieved at certain intervals.

Have you ever watched a group of children ages two through five? If so, you know they often behave quite differently. A child of two, for example, is happy to play by himself while a five year old enjoys being involved with other children. What accounts for this variation? Each child is at a different stage in his growth and development pattern.

As a child matures, he passes through certain stages of physical, mental, emotional, social and spiritual development. These stages of development follow a recognizable pattern. Even though each child develops at his own speed, it is possible to predict, generally, how he will respond at a specific age. And more important, it is possible to understand WHY he will respond a certain way at that given age.

Specific behavior traits are evident at each stage of development. It is necessary for the adult who works with young children to understand the behavior traits of the age level with which he works. Then he can gear learning activities to the child's abilities and know what response to expect from the child.

Let's explore some of the behavior traits that affect the planning and procedures of the adult who works with two year old children.

THE TWO YEAR OLD'S BODY DEMANDS EXERCISE.

How wonderfully God has made the young child! He is constantly on the move—running, jumping, and climbing. Because the large muscles in his legs and arms are developing, he's not quite sure of his balance. He tumbles often. Plan for open spaces in your room in which the child is free to move. Keep furnishings at a minimum. Provide equipment such as a rocking boat and climbing steps that allow him to use his large muscles. Use simple finger fun activity and songs that allow him to reach and stretch, to jump and clap.

THE TWO YEAR OLD'S SMALL MUSCLES ARE NOT YET DEVELOPED.

Small muscles are those in his hands that will eventually enable him to control a pencil or scissors. For draw-n-color activities, provide large sheets of blank paper and jumbo crayons. (Do NOT expect a child under six to color within an outline!) Provide puzzles with a few large pieces; have large spools or beads to string. Provide large blocks or cartons he can stack and manipulate.

THE TWO YEAR OLD'S INTEREST SPAN IS SHORT.

Expect him to pick up a toy, drop it and move on to something else. He is likely to participate briefly in one activity and then move to another. He prefers to play alone. Two children may play side by side, but each will be involved in his own activity, showing little interest in the activity of the other. Provide a variety of activities of interest to twos. Do not expect a child to remain interested in any one thing for more than a few minutes.

THE TWO YEAR OLD TIRES EASILY.

His constant activity is a source of real fatigue which is often the cause of his unacceptable behavior. He doesn't know how to stop and rest. Provide alternating times of active and quiet play; be alert to the child who needs to "slow down." Gently redirect his attention to looking at a book or working a puzzle with you. During the second hour of your morning schedule include a rest time. For specific suggestions see your *Leader's/Teacher's Manual.*

For example, Mrs. Cook watched as Nancy prepared to feed her doll at the home living area. She knew Nancy had been very active all morning and she noticed that Nancy was beginning to hit children who came too near. Just as Mrs. Cook reached the table, Paul took one of Nancy's dishes. "Mine!" Nancy shouted as she grabbed the dish from Paul.

Mrs. Cook gave Paul other dishes to use. She waited a few moments while Nancy fed her doll. Then she said, "Nancy, your baby has had a good lunch. I think she'd like to hear a story. I have a new book she will like." Gently, she took Nancy and her doll to a quiet corner and together they looked at a picture book. As they sat quietly talking about the pictures, Nancy began to relax and was soon able to join the other children.

THE TWO YEAR OLD SAYS "NO" WHEN HE FREQUENTLY MEANS "YES."

Because he is on the move and is curious about everything, the word a two year old hears most frequently is "no!" He often uses the word himself because of its simplicity and familiarity. Phrase your suggestions in the form of statements rather than questions. Avoid, "Do you want to . . . ?" Rather say, "Please bring the book to me. . . . Thank you, Tom."

THE TWO YEAR OLD LIKES TO ATTEMPT TO DO THINGS FOR HIMSELF.

His frequent plea is "Let me do it!" Offer assistance only as needed. However, step in before he becomes frustrated. Suggest ways he can accomplish at least part of the task himself. Then praise his successful attempts. Provide materials and equipment he can easily manage.

THE TWO YEAR OLD'S VOCABULARY IS INCREASING.
However, he uses more words than he understands. He enjoys listening to songs, finger fun and rhythms; he likes to hear his favorites over and over again. When talking with the two year old use simple words that mean what they say. Avoid symbolism! Speak slowly and in short sentences. Expect a two year old's initial response to be one of observation. He enjoys listening to you sing, repeat action songs, tell brief stories, etc. Use his favorite songs, finger fun and stories again and again.

THE TWO YEAR OLD IS BECOMING AWARE OF HIMSELF AS A PERSON.
Everything he does relates to himself. Sing songs that include his name, such as, "Who made Danny? God did. . . ."[2] Use his name often in your conversation. When he talks to you, look into his face and give him your undivided attention. Let him feel that, at least for that moment, he is the most important person in the room to you. Plan activities and provide equipment whereby he can experience success. Offer words of praise and encouragement as you refer to his specific actions.

THE TWO YEAR OLD HAS LITTLE REGARD FOR THE RIGHTS OF OTHERS.
At times it seems as if no and mine are the only words he knows! Sharing and taking turns are new words and new ideas to most twos. When disputes occur, a two will more likely respond to distraction rather than reasoning. "Chris, that's Eric's truck. Here is a red truck for you to use." Provide duplicates of favorite toys.

THE TWO YEAR OLD HAS LITTLE SENSE OF TIME.
He can't be hurried. Do not expect an immediate response to your requests. Allow plenty of time for mov-

ing from one part of the schedule to the next; for putting on coats, for wash-up and toileting details.

THE TWO YEAR OLD SEEKS CLOSE PHYSICAL CONTACT WITH LOVING, UNDERSTANDING ADULTS.

Jesus called little children to Him and rebuked those who would send them away. We can easily imagine that He held them on His lap and listened patiently to their chatter. Those who guide twos need to be kind, patient Christians who love little children and who are willing to give the kind of help the child's behavior shows he needs. A smile and a friendly pat might meet the needs of one child while a hug or a few moments of cuddling might be the answer for another. An effective teacher knows the needs of the children and is able to respond to these needs.

THE TWO YEAR OLD IMITATES THE WORDS AND ACTIONS OF THOSE AROUND HIM.

Provide an example of positive behavior as you guide children's activities and as you relate to other adults in the room. Use the same good manners with children as you do with adults. Children deserve to hear "please" when a request is made of them and "thank you" when the job is done.

THE TWO YEAR OLD'S MOMENTS OF FEAR, DISAPPOINTMENT AND FRUSTRATION REQUIRE THE HELP OF AN UNDERSTANDING ADULT.

Should a child cry when his mother leaves, avoid shaming him. Help him feel secure by giving him personal attention, such as showing him a toy or a book. Ask his mother to leave something, such as gloves or a scarf to help assure the child she will return.

During an activity be alert for any child who might be reaching the point of frustration. Step in with a suggestion to help him succeed. "Jan, your puzzle has a pretty flower in it. I wonder if this piece will fit here."

A child is born to grow and to learn. While these stages of growth do follow a certain pattern, each child develops at his own speed. Each child is an individual whose growth and development are influenced by his health, his temperament, his interests, his family and friends. One two year old might have the behavior traits of a three year old while another might act like a one year old. Still another child might be mature in some areas and immature in others.

Remember that each child is a special person—an individual created and loved by God. It is the teacher's responsibility to know what makes that special person "tick."

THE TWO YEAR OLD IS AN EXPLORER RATHER THAN A CREATOR.

Because he learns through his senses, he curiously pokes, feels, hits, tastes, listens to and smells the world about him. Peter was watching the fish at the God's Wonders table. Suddenly, water was splashing everywhere as Peter's hand went into the water and after the fish. Mr. Clark gently removed Peter's hand from the bowl. As he dried Peter and the table top, he said, "God made goldfish for us to look at. Not to touch. Watch the fish's tail move as he swims." As they watched together, Mr. Clark sang, "Who made the goldfish? God did. . . ."[2] Mr. Clark knew Peter was not being "bad." He was simply attempting to satisfy his curiosity about the fish.

To stimulate and help satisfy this curiosity, provide equipment and materials that invite investigation; remove breakable "for-teacher-use-only" materials from your room. Other children are usually a source of wonder to a two year old. He frequently treats them as physical objects, pushing or hitting them with whatever is at hand. Be alert to the physical safety of children at all times.

STOP! Before you continue, do these two things:

1   *Plan a learning activity for next Sunday based on the fact that a two year old's growing body demands exercise. Select an activity appropriate to the lesson's Bible teaching/learning aim given in your* Leader's/Teacher's Manual.

2   *List several ways you can help a child be-*
    come aware of himself as a person. Include
    at least one finger fun or song in which you
    can insert the child's name or the child can
    use the personal pronoun "I." Learn the
    finger fun or song to use next Sunday. At
    the close of the Sunday school period review
    your list and see how many of the sugges-
    tions you used.

WHAT CAN A TWO YEAR OLD LEARN?

When does a child begin to learn? Is there some magical moment when something clicks in his head and learning begins? No, at the moment of a child's birth the potential for learning is present and continues throughout his life.

THE TWO YEAR OLD CAN LEARN ABOUT GOD.

He can know God made him; that God made his world; that God loves him. To help the child grasp and retain these basic scriptural truths, make use of his natural curiosity. Provide objects he can touch and smell, such as rocks, leaves, flowers and pinecones. In conversation guide him to know "God made the rock" or "God made your nose so you can smell the pretty flower."

Also provide an environment in which he can relive experiences that are familiar to him. For example, Mr. Martin remained close by and watched as Allen played in the home living area. Allen sat down at the small table and pretended to eat. Mr. Martin sat down on the floor beside him and said, "God made your good food to grow. God loves you." Mr. Martin was alert for opportunities to remind Allen in a simple way of God's love.

Use stories, pictures and conversation to help the child sense God's love through His plan for provision of food, of care through parents and adults.

The child can know he can talk to God; that prayer is talking to God. Help him learn to phrase simple prayers of thanks to God (Jesus) for specific things, such as "Thank you, God, for our juice." Pray simply, using familiar words that mean what they say.

There are many opportunities during the hour for prayer, so do not restrict your prayers only to specially designated times, such as before a snack. At the God's Wonders table when prayer seems a natural response to observing a bowl of fish, you might pray, "Thank you, God, for making fish." While the children are playing with dough, the teacher might sing softly, "Thank you, God. I thank you, God. Thank you, God, for Scott's hands."[2]

THE TWO YEAR OLD CAN LEARN ABOUT JESUS.

He can know that Jesus is his special friend, that Jesus loves him. Use Bible Thoughts, songs, pictures and stories repeatedly to assure him of Jesus' continuous love.

Miss Jones showed a large, colorful picture of Jesus to several children. Sally, attracted by the activity, came over, pointed at the picture and said, "Jesus!"

"That's right, Sally," Miss Jones replied. "This is a picture of Jesus. Jesus is our friend." Miss Jones began to sing, "Jesus is my best friend. Jesus is my best friend." Later, Miss Jones posted the picture at the child's eye level on the bulletin board.

THE TWO YEAR OLD CAN LEARN ABOUT THE BIBLE.

He can know the Bible is a special book that tells about God and Jesus. Refer to the Bible as the source of your stories and Bible Thoughts. Always have the Bible open nearby as you tell the Bible story. The department Picture Bible[3] should be on display. A teacher nearby helps to insure careful handling and helps the child understand that the Bible is a special book. "Our Bible is a special book, Tommy. Our Bible tells us about Jesus. Here is a picture of Jesus helping His friends."

THE TWO YEAR OLD CAN LEARN ABOUT HIS CHURCH.

He can know his church is a special place where he learns about Jesus and God. Use phrases such as, "Here in our church we. . . ." to remind the child where he is.

Church is often one of the first places a two year old goes away from his home. He most likely will need reassurance as he adjusts to new faces and unfamiliar surroundings. Help him know his church is a special place where friendly adults plan pleasant experiences for him; where they look forward to his coming. Help him to feel happy and "at home" when he comes to church. Help him to go home feeling "I'm glad I came. I want to come again."

Everything and everyone in your room—the attitude and sincerity of the teachers, the room arrangement, the activities—can encourage or discourage this feeling of well-being. If the child comes into a cluttered room where the teachers are unprepared or disinterested, he will probably feel insecure and frightened. However, if the child comes into an attractive room where appropriate activity materials are ready, where the teacher's smile is friendly and her interest in him is sincere, he will probably feel secure, at ease and glad he came. The very fact that you are prepared when the first child arrives shows that you are interested in him. Use words such as *we, our, let's* to give the child a sense of belonging.

THE TWO YEAR OLD CAN DEVELOP LOVING ATTITUDES TOWARD OTHERS.

He can grow toward feelings and actions that reflect Christian ideals as expressed in Scripture. A child generally reflects the love he has experienced in his relationships with those who love him. He learns to love by being loved. A child learns to be kind by experiencing kindness from someone else. It's as simple as that! For approximately an hour (or two) on Sunday morning YOU are the example. It is your love and your kindness he will experience and then reflect.

A two year old is pretty much a "loner." He is happy to play by himself. Often it will look as if he is playing with another child, but closer observation will reveal that he is actually involved in parallel play. This simply means he is playing next to another child and possibly using some of the same materials, but he is still involved in his own activity. To help a child relate to others, offer opportunities for interaction.

For example, Mrs. Adams sat down on the floor with a dump-n-fill bucket filled with large, brightly colored spools. A few children sat down beside her as she dumped the spools onto the rug. She dropped a spool back into the bucket. "I put a red spool in the bucket," she said. "Now Cathy can put a spool in the bucket." Mrs. Adams guided the activity so one spool was dropped in at a time and each child waited his turn. "Now it's Kenny's turn. . . . Kenny, put in a pretty green spool. . . . It's your turn again, Cathy." Soon the bucket was filled again.

Call attention to another child's work. "Look at Jack's building. He did a fine job with the blocks today. . . . Cindy is taking good care of her baby."

When a child does exhibit acceptable behavior toward another child, be ready with words of praise and encouragement. "Billy, thank you for helping Jack with that block. Sharon, thank you for moving over. Now Sally has a place to sit, too. You are a kind helper."

THE TWO YEAR OLD CAN LEARN ABOUT HIMSELF.

He can grow toward developing a sense of adequacy. To help him feel that he is important as an individual, offer genuine praise for his accomplishments. Praise his successful efforts with your words, your smile, or a friendly pat. Take time to listen to what he has to say no matter how trivial it might seem. Bend or sit down on his eye level; give him your undivided attention.

The child can begin to learn to solve problems with materials. Offer opportunities for a child to experience success by providing materials and equipment he can easily manage. Stay close by to offer guidance and help when needed. Be alert to step in before he becomes frustrated; yet allow him the freedom necessary to achieve a measure of independence.

The two year old comes to you on Sunday morning with the potential to learn about God, Jesus, the Bible, his church, others and himself. He can learn simple facts; he can develop attitudes and feelings that will serve as a foundation for his spiritual growth.

STOP! *Before you continue:*

Read your Bible teaching/learning aim for your current unit and lesson in your Leader's/Teacher's Manual. Now carefully read through your lesson material for next Sunday; list four ways you feel this aim is effectively accomplished.

For instance, if your aim involves helping the child to name and demonstrate ways of kindness, the Bible learning activities (Step 1) should offer him the opportunities to do these things. The other parts of the lesson (Moments of Worship, Bible Story/Activity Time) should also provide additional opportunities.

CHAPTER THREE

THE THREE YEAR OLD

God has entrusted you, leader and teacher, with the responsibility and opportunity to help the young child learn some vital and basic scriptural truths. To help him learn these scriptural truths effectively, those who guide him must be aware of his pattern of growth and development and the accompanying behavior traits or characteristics.

There is a wide range of differences among children. Each child is an individual and develops at his own rate. His rate of growth is determined by many factors, including health and environment. However, there is enough similarity among children of the same age that specific characteristics can be noted. These behavior traits or characteristics should be used as a guide when planning learning activities for the child; they should never be used as a mold in which to place every child when he reaches his third birthday.

Let's look briefly at the behavior of a typical three year old child.

THE THREE YEAR OLD IS DEVELOPING LARGE MUSCLE CONTROL.

He's sure on his feet. Provide activities and materials, such as blocks for building, that encourage the use of his large muscles. Provide dough to squeeze and pound; large crayons and sheets of blank paper for draw-n-color activities. He needs room in which to move about. Keep furnishings to a minimum. Provide a choice of activities and freedom to move from one activity to another.

The three year old's small muscles are not yet fully developed. He cannot be expected to cut accurately with scissors, or to color within an outline.

THE THREE YEAR OLD PLAYS HARD AND TIRES EASILY.

Alternate periods of active and quiet play. Be alert to the child who is becoming overstimulated. Guide him to a quiet activity, such as working a puzzle or looking at a picture book with you. During the second hour of your morning schedule, plan for a rest time of not less than ten minutes. See your *Leader's/Teacher's Manual* for detailed suggestions.

THE THREE YEAR OLD IS ATTENTIVE ONLY AS LONG AS HE IS INTERESTED.

His attention span is limited. Alternate listening times with more active experiences. Use songs and finger fun that allow the child to move. Because of his limited experiences, he needs to see—and often touch—lesson-related pictures and objects. As Mrs. Graham told a story of ways God planned for food to grow, she noticed that some of the children were becoming restless. Without stopping her story, she said, "And God planned for apples to grow on trees. Let's pretend we are apple trees and stretch our branches way up into the sky. . . . Let's pretend the wind is blowing our branches. . . ." As the children moved their arms high overhead, she sang, "The apple trees are swaying. . . ."[1] When the song ended and everyone sat down again, she showed a food picture and continued her story by saying, "Look what else God made that's good to eat!"

Mrs. Graham recognized two needs: (1) the children's need to stretch and move, and (2) her need to regain the children's attention. Both needs were met by giving the children an opportunity to sing and move. They were actively participating in the story. The second need was met by drawing the children's attention directly to the picture.

A three year old does not understand symbolism! Use simple stories told in literal terms—words that mean exactly what they say. His memory is undependable. Avoid asking, "What was last Sunday's story about?" He also may have difficulty understanding directions. Give one brief direction at a time. Allow the child to complete the task before suggesting the next one.

THE THREE YEAR OLD
IS SENSITIVE TO YOUR ACTIONS,
ATTITUDES AND FEELINGS.

Know each child as an individual. Jesus was keenly aware of people as individuals. Scripture recounts again and again incidents in which Jesus singled out one person who had a special need for His loving-kindness. For instance, when Jesus was surrounded by throngs who had come to see Him, He stopped and called Zacchaeus—by name![2] Nothing should be clearer to the Christian than the value of each one of us in the sight of the Lord. It was His love and concern for each of us personally that sent Him to the cross. You represent God's love to the young child. As you express a genuine interest in him as an individual, you are vividly communicating God's love in a way the young child can understand.

Use the child's name often as you talk with him. Listen attentively to what he tells you. Scott was trying earnestly to tell his teacher something he considered of great importance. His teacher kept on preparing materials for another part of the morning schedule, occasionally offering a noncommittal "uh-huh." Finally, in desperation Scott said, "Listen to me!"

"I AM listening," his teacher replied.

"But you're not listening with your face!" was Scott's comment.

Scott in his three year old way distinguished between having someone merely hear his words and someone listen to him attentively. When you talk with a child, sit or bend down so you are at his eye level, give him your undivided attention (stop what you are doing), respond to his words appropriately by sharing his enthusiasm or offering a bit of sympathy. As you show genuine interest in each child, you are demonstrating God's love in a way the child can understand. The Lord Jesus' command that we *love one another*[3] becomes alive with meaning. God's Word demonstrated is often more convincing to young children than God's Word explained.

The young child is keenly aware of the way you handle your Bible, your attitude of prayer and your enthusiasm as you help him know what God's Word says. Your respect and reverence toward the Bible helps lay the foundation for the child's developing attitudes and feelings toward God's Word.

THE THREE YEAR OLD ENJOYS BEING WITH OTHER CHILDREN BUT STILL LIKES TO PLAY ALONE.

He hasn't quite left his self-centered "me, my and mine" world. Offer activities that allow him to participate successfully with other children. To help him enjoy his own accomplishments, provide tasks within his abilities. Help strengthen his feelings of self-worth by offering words of genuine praise for his efforts.

Overaggressiveness is noticeable in some three year olds. Sometimes this behavior is the child's way to gain the attention of adults or other children. Sometimes it's simply a child's lack of experience in working with children his own age. Plan for each child to have some individual attention during the morning. Also create opportunities that foster social development. For instance, "Terry, you have lots of pegs. I think John needs more pegs. What can you do to help John? . . . You are a kind friend to share pegs with John."

THE THREE YEAR OLD IS TRUSTING AND READY TO ACCEPT WHAT YOU TELL HIM ABOUT GOD AND THE LORD JESUS.

In conversation and song use Bible truths to assure him of God's (Jesus') love and care for him. As Sam and his family rode along home from church, Sam announced, "God didn't come to Sunday school today." After a moment of silence, he added, "But He sent my teacher." To the young child, you represent God's love. Your actions, attitudes and words reflect His love. As the child experiences your love, he can more readily understand and accept God's love. Help the child to know God made him and that God loves him. Help him to know Jesus as a kind, loving friend.

When the three year old comes to church, he brings all of himself. He brings a child who is fearfully and wonderfully made; a child who grows in his own way and at his own rate—just as God has planned.

> **STOP!** Before you continue, list three activities in which a three year old can successfully work with other children. List three activities at which he can work independently. Use your Leader's/Teacher's Manual as a reference.

WHAT CAN A THREE YEAR OLD LEARN?

Specialists in early childhood research assure us that almost every young child possesses an inherent ability to learn. To help him use this natural ability, we need to recognize just what he's ready to learn; then provide an environment and experiences that are appropriate to his stage of development.

THE THREE YEAR OLD CAN LEARN ABOUT GOD.

He is capable of knowing that God made him and loves him. Use phrases such as "God loves you" and "God cares about you" often in your conversation. Then show the child through your attitudes and actions what these phrases mean. A child can understand more fully the meaning of God's love as he feels and experiences loving concern from understanding adults.

A child can know only as much about God as the adults around him care to reveal. Use Bible Thoughts and Bible stories to illustrate God as creator and to assure the child of God's continuing and unconditional love.

The child can know that he can talk to God; that prayer is talking to God. Be aware of the many opportunities for prayer during your Sunday morning schedule. Do not restrict your prayers only to specified times. For instance, as several children used the touch-n-feel box, Mrs. Wallis asked, "What are you using to feel the things in our box? . . . We can tell

God thank you for our hands." **Mrs. Wallis** began to sing, "Thank you, God. I thank you, God. Thank you, God, for Mary's hands."[1] She repeated the prayer song several times during the activity.

Pray simple prayers of thanks to God (Jesus) for specific people and things, such as "Thank you, God, for our friend Patty." Use brief phrases and familiar words that mean what they say.

THE THREE YEAR OLD CAN LEARN ABOUT JESUS.

He can know that Jesus is the baby whose birth we celebrate at Christmas—that Christmas is Jesus' birthday. Draw parallels between the child's experiences and those of the child Jesus. "Were you ever a tiny baby? . . . Are you growing? . . . Do you help Mommy and Daddy?" Such comparisons help the child relate to Jesus as a person.

A young child acts and reacts primarily on a feeling level. His feelings about Jesus can include love. The child can grow in his love for Jesus as his knowledge about Jesus increases and as he sees Jesus' love reflected in the attitudes and actions of adults. He can know Jesus is a special person; a special friend and helper.

A three year old can know Jesus loved and helped people and that Jesus loves and helps him. The child finds security in this knowledge. Some unexpected confusion at home had caused Cathy to feel insecure about staying in Sunday school one Sunday. As her father left with a hasty promise that "Mommy and I will be back soon," Cathy looked very sad, indeed.

Miss Payne sat down to comfort her, but before Miss Payne could speak, Cathy said, "I want to sing a song about Jesus."

Miss Payne took Cathy's hand and began to sing, "Jesus loves me, Jesus loves me. Jesus loves me every day. . . ."[1] When the song ended, Miss Payne said, "Jesus loves you, Cathy."

Cathy smiled and said, "Jesus loves me." Reassured of Jesus' love, Cathy joined the other children at an activity.

Use Bible stories, Bible Thoughts, songs and pictures to help the three year old know of Jesus' kind and loving deeds and to assure and reassure him of Jesus' continuing love.

THE THREE YEAR OLD CAN LEARN ABOUT THE BIBLE.

The child needs to see the Bible in use so he will recognize it as the book from which he learns about God and the Lord Jesus. As his teacher opened her Bible to begin her story, Billy moved closer and said, "Show me Jesus." The teacher opened her Bible to the picture of Jesus she had carefully taped inside the front cover and she said,

> "We open our Bible.
> What do we see?
> A picture of Jesus!
> He loves you and me."

The Bible stories selected for your *Leader's/Teacher's Manual* are those of interest to a young child. Show him where the story is found in the Bible. Children enjoy hearing the same story again and again. Identify Bible words in your natural conversation. . . . "The Bible tells us to *love one another.*"

Be sure the songs you sing are biblically accurate. Avoid songs that use words beyond the understanding of a three year old or songs that include symbolism, such as "This Little Light of Mine."

The attitude and feeling a child develops about the Bible reflect the attitude and feeling he sees you display. When you enthusiastically present God's Word in ways he can understand; when you relate its message to his own interest and activities, then he will come to feel God's Word is important and meaningful to him.

THE THREE YEAR OLD CAN LEARN ABOUT HIS CHURCH.

He can think of the church as a place where he is wanted and loved. "My church" to a young child is usually his Sunday school room. A three year old was talking with an adult in front of the church one Sunday morning. "Where are you going?" he asked.

The adult pointed toward the sanctuary and answered, "I'm going to church."

The three year old pointed toward the Christian education building and with a happy smile replied, "THAT'S my church!"

Help the child associate happy feelings with his church. He has many years (hopefully) of Sunday school attendance ahead of him. It is especially important that these initial experiences be pleasant ones. Help the child feel the church is a place where he feels and receives love; where understanding adults look forward to his coming each week; where he has pleasant experiences. Through your attitudes and actions, help him know and feel you are glad he comes to church.

The planning and preparation that takes place before Sunday morning is vitally important to the child's reaction to his Sunday school experience. The importance of being ready when the first child arrives cannot be overemphasized! A neat and uncluttered room, materials that are ready for use and relaxed, prepared teachers show the child that you care about him. Satisfying experiences help the child feel "I like it here. I'm glad I came."

Use words such as *we, our church* and *let's* to give the child a sense of belonging. Avoid using the term "God's house." It is confusing to a child who thinks of a house as someone's home.

THE THREE YEAR OLD CAN DEVELOP LOVING ATTITUDES TOWARD OTHERS.

Young children are naturally self-centered. However, as a three year old makes the transition from solitary play into friendships, he can begin to recognize the needs and rights of others. Adults may talk about sharing, being kind and loving until they are numb. But only as the child experiences these actions (as he feels them bestowed or as he gives them) will they become his way of living. This kind of growth requires a climate of frequent forgiveness and fresh beginnings. Provide activities that allow children to relate to one another. Identify and interpret specific acts of kindness so a child knows what to do to be loving and friendly. Be ready with words of praise and encouragement when a child exhibits acceptable behavior toward another child. Help a child who has had an unhappy experience with another child get started in a new activity.

Sharing and taking turns are new ideas to most three year olds. Identify what these words mean. "First Mary can play with the doll; then Sue can play with it. That's taking turns." A concerned teacher will be sure that Sue gets her turn so she will not conclude that taking turns means losing out.

A child also learns by observing and imitating your actions toward others. By watching your acts of kindness he can begin to understand how to show kindness to others. Teachers provide an example of Christian love and concern by their actions and reactions in the department.

THE THREE YEAR OLD CAN LEARN ABOUT HIMSELF.

Before a child can relate satisfactorily to others, he needs to feel good about himself. Help him develop self-confidence and a good self-image. This is not conceit. It is the concept of self the Lord Jesus used when He gave His new commandment, *Love your neighbor as yourself.*[4] Provide experiences in which each child can succeed. Allow him the freedom necessary to achieve a measure of independence; yet be sensitive enough to step in before he becomes frustrated. Offer words of praise and encouragement.

God made each child an individual, different from all others. Appreciate that each one is precious in the sight of God. Value the child for who he is. Help him feel he is important. To a three year old a hug, a pat on the shoulder or a friendly smile can mean "I like you. You're special." Help him feel loved and secure. Use his name often. Use songs and finger fun in which you can insert the child's name or the child can use the personal pronoun "I".

> *STOP! Before you continue, list three ways your Leader's/Teacher's Manual suggests that you can help a child learn of God; the Lord Jesus; the Bible.*

CHAPTER FOUR

THE FOUR YEAR OLD

The Bible tells us that *Jesus grew both tall and wise, and was loved by God and man.*[1] Jesus came to earth not as a man, but as a baby who grew just as a young child grows today. He was a Two who wanted to do things for Himself, a Three with a short attention span and a never-still-a-minute Four. Jesus was unique not just because He was God, but because He was a child with His own abilities and needs, growing at His own rate—just as God planned.

What are these never-still-a-minute four year olds like? One thing of which we are certain, no two children develop at exactly the same rate and exactly the same way. A child's interests, his abilities and his needs make him different from every other child. Each child has his own inner timetable. God planned it so.

While each child is different and grows at his own rate, he still follows a certain general pattern of growth and development. Specific characteristics evident in this pattern of development make it possible to generally predict how a child will respond at a certain age. Adults who guide four year olds should be familiar with these characteristics in order to plan successful learning experiences within the child's abilities and interests.

THE FOUR YEAR OLD IS IN A PERIOD OF RAPID
PHYSICAL GROWTH.

His coordination has improved and he is stronger and more confident than he was at three. He seems to be constantly on the go—running, jumping, walking or climbing. His rapidly developing large muscles need exercise. Plan open spaces in your room so he can move about freely. Encourage freehand draw-n-color activities using large sheets of paper. (Do not expect a four year old to color within lines!) At the paint easel he uses his large brush to make sweeping strokes of bright color. Provide manipulative equipment, such as puzzles, blocks and construction toys to assemble. Provide salt/flour dough or Play Doh for the child to squeeze and pound. Use finger fun, action songs, rhythm activities and *simple* story play.

The four year old is gaining in his control of small muscles. Although his use of these muscles is still often undependable, he enjoys attempting activities that involve fine coordination. Provide opportunities for him to button, zip a zipper, lace shoes and cut on a line.

The four year old tires quickly. His rapid growth and constant activity cause him to become easily fatigued. His tiredness may result in unacceptable behavior. Be alert to a child who is becoming overstimulated. Redirect his attention to a quiet activity, such as working with dough or looking at a book. Alternate times of active and quiet play throughout your morning schedule.

THE FOUR YEAR OLD HAS A STRONG DESIRE TO LEARN. He is curious and questioning. His favorite words seem to be *how, what* and *why*. He enjoys experimenting with words. Making up silly-sounding rhymes is great fun for him. He continues his learning in much the same way as when he was three—by doing. Provide materials he can touch, smell, see and even taste. Use lesson-related objects and activities to relate Scripture truths to the child's life. Use simple words and literal phrases that mean exactly what they say. The four year old does not understand words that are symbolistic. For instance, when a child hears "Ask Jesus into your heart" he thinks of his own physical heart.

The four year old can now concentrate for longer

periods of time than when he was three. However, his attention span is still short—about five or six minutes. His rapidly developing large muscles make it difficult for him to sit still for long periods. Provide a variety of activities and materials. Allow him the freedom to move from one activity to another. Seeing the same materials Sunday after Sunday causes a child to lose interest. Plan new activities frequently, appropriate to your lesson's Bible teaching/learning aim.

The four year old is learning to enjoy participating with other children in group activities. Again, because of his limited attention span, the activities should be kept brief. He enjoys simple stories and group singing.

THE FOUR YEAR OLD IS TESTING HIS WORLD.

He may exhibit unacceptable behavior just to see how far he can go. He finds security in the very limits he defies; yet he needs the security of limits that do not hinder his freedom to experiment. Be consistent in your every-Sunday guidances. Be positive in your suggestions. Emphasize the behavior you desire rather than the kind you want to discourage. Say, "We keep the blocks in the block area" rather than "Don't bring the blocks to the home corner!" The word "don't" often makes a child want to resist. Often he is overaggressive and may use physical force to get what he wants. Be alert to the physical safety of all the children.

The four year old seems overly sure of his abilities. He brags and boasts about himself. "I can climb to the very top of this building; I can run faster than anyone else." Do not dispute his claims, but redirect his conversation. "You can run and jump because your legs are growing strong, just as God planned. I need a strong boy like you to help put these blocks away."

THE FOUR YEAR OLD IS SENSITIVE TO THE FEELINGS AND ATTITUDES OF THE ADULTS ABOUT HIM.

He longs for and actively seeks adult approval. He responds to friendliness and wants to be loved, especially by his teacher. Show interest in him as an individual. Be interested in what interests him and in what he has to say. Be ready with a friendly greeting, a smile or a gentle pat. "That's a pretty orange shirt you're wearing, Kevin. Is it new? . . . I like the stripes." Give him praise and recognition when he exhibits acceptable behavior. Work with him in small informal groups that allow maximum personal attention.

THE FOUR YEAR OLD SHOWS A GROWING INTEREST IN DOING THINGS WITH OTHER CHILDREN.

He is beginning to think of himself as one person among many. He prefers to work in small groups. (Younger fours may still prefer to work alone.) Provide activities that allow the child to work in groups of two or three children.

The four year old likes to pretend. "I'm the daddy and you're the mother" kinds of play occur frequently in the home living area. He also likes to play out his experiences. "We're going to the park today. Everybody get ready," a four is likely to announce. Provide adult clothing for dress-up. Include scarves, hats, jewelry, vases, etc. for dramatic play. Encourage male-oriented play by providing materials men might use such as a discarded camera, binoculars, keys, men's hats, etc.

Moving out into a world of new friends, new activities and experiences, new relationships with adults, means these children need your help. Your thoughtful and careful guidance can help assure their success.

STOP! Before you continue:

> *On a piece of paper write the names of two children in your class. In terms of the characteristics you have just read, list the ways in which these two children are alike and how they are different at this stage of their development.*

WHAT CAN A FOUR YEAR OLD LEARN?

Every normal child is born with the potential to grow and to learn. We want him to *become more and more in every way like Christ.*[2] To help him grow, we plan experiences appropriate to the child's specific needs and learning capabilities.

THE FOUR YEAR OLD CAN LEARN ABOUT GOD.

He can know God made him and loves him. But to begin to understand God's love, a child must first feel and experience love. In your conversation use phrases such as "God loves you" and "God cares about you." Then show the child through your actions what these phrases mean. God so often demonstrates His love to little ones through concerned adults.

Never use God as an instrument of correction. "God won't love you if you kick over Jerry's blocks," certainly is a misguided interpretation of the Christian faith! True, God disapproves of thoughtless and selfish actions. However, the moment of a child's misbehavior is not the appropriate time to help a child learn of God's disapproval. Select a time when things are going well to help a child know that while God does not like some things we do, He still loves us.

Answer the child's questions about God truthfully and concisely. A child will often lose interest if you attempt to give him lengthy explanations. Use the Bible stories in your *Leader's/Teacher's Manual* to illustrate God as creator and to reassure the child of God's love. These special units about God contain a variety of experiences that say the same thing in many ways to the child.

The four year old can know that he can talk to God; that praying is talking to God. There are many opportunities throughout the morning for spontaneous prayers. Do not restrict your prayers to specific times. Pray simply in words young children can understand.

The four year old can begin to offer his own simple prayers. Guide him in phrasing prayers in his own words. Help him to know prayer is a way he can express love for God and for the Lord Jesus.

Mrs. Palmer remained nearby as the children played in the home living area. She watched as they set the table for a pretend meal. As the children sat down to eat she said, "What do we do before we eat? John is the daddy in this family. He can tell God thank you for the good food." If John had been reluctant to pray, Mrs. Palmer would have prayed simply, "Thank you, God, for our good food. In Jesus' name, Amen."

THE FOUR YEAR OLD CAN LEARN ABOUT JESUS.

He can know Jesus as the baby whose birth we celebrate at Christmas. He can know that Jesus grew just
as he is growing. Draw parallels between Jesus' early
years and that of the child. "Jesus grew and grew just
as you are. . . . Jesus helped Joseph and Mary just
like you help your family."

The four year old can know Jesus as a special person—a kind helper and friend. He can know God
wants us to do the things Jesus said. He can know
that stories of Jesus are found in the Bible. As you tell
stories of Jesus' miraculous deeds, emphasize Jesus'
desire to help others, rather than the miracles themselves. Make clear that because Jesus loved His
friends, He helped them in many wonderful ways.
Direct the child's thoughts to what Jesus did and said.
Encourage the child to do friendly things for others.
Plan situations, such as drawing pictures for a sick
friend or arranging a bouquet for the minister so the
child can have firsthand experiences in showing
loving-kindness. Recognize his acts of kindness. "You
are very kind to give Sally some clay, Chris. Jesus
was kind to His friends, too."

The child's feelings and love for Jesus grow from
his knowledge. However, his feelings also grow from
observing the attitudes adults show toward Jesus.
The child absorbs your feelings as you talk with him
about Jesus. Think of the responsibility this places on
you, teacher! Stop now and consider your personal
relationship with Jesus Christ. What feelings about
Jesus do you reveal to the four year olds you teach?

THE FOUR YEAR OLD CAN LEARN ABOUT THE BIBLE.

He can know that the Bible tells us about Jesus and
how Jesus wants us to live. In your natural conversation, identify Bible words. . . "Our Bible says *God
cares about you.*"

Keep a Bible in various areas of the room for quick
identification of Bible words. Underline Bible words
with red pencil. Show the child where a favorite story
is found in the Bible. Let him "read" Bible Thoughts
directly from the Bible. "See these words I've marked,

Tony? These words say, *'Be . . . kind.'* You can help me read the Bible words." To help the child recognize where familiar Bible stories are located, make a Picture Bible. With cellophane insert the pictures from the child's Bible storybook near the Scripture passages they illustrate. Use a red pen to lightly shade the verses that tell of each Bible story picture. The child can find familiar pictures and "read" the Bible story shaded in red.

The four year old observes how you handle the Bible and your tone of voice as you talk about the Bible. The child understands best what he sees and experiences, so the attitudes he forms about the Bible are largely a result of watching adults. How important is the Bible to you? Do you refer in a natural way to what God's Word says? Do you tell Bible stories with interest and enthusiasm?

THE FOUR YEAR OLD CAN LEARN ABOUT THE CHURCH.

He can learn to think of the church as a pleasant place where he is welcomed and respected. To the four year old his "church" is usually his Sunday school room. His first impressions are formed when he first enters the room. Be ready with a warm, personal greeting. Bend down or sit at his eye level; use his name often as you speak to him. Have a variety of activities planned that will meet his needs and interests.

When you refer to the church avoid the term "God's house." Because a young child is literal minded, he thinks of a house as a place where a person lives. "I'm here in God's house, but where is God?" might be a child's natural conclusion.

To help him think of the church as more than just his department, the child needs to see other parts of the church building. Take a few children at a time to visit the sanctuary. To make this a profitable learning experience, plan ahead. Tell children where they are going; what they will be seeing and something to look for. Let them sit in the pews; show them the pulpit Bible. Point out the choir loft, organ, windows, etc. Encourage questions. When you return to the classroom, talk about what they have seen.

Invite your minister to visit in the department. Talk with him ahead of time to remind him of children's interests and activities.

THE FOUR YEAR OLD CAN DEVELOP LOVING ATTITUDES TOWARD OTHERS.

Friends are becoming increasingly important to him. He wants to work and play with a few other children. But he often needs help in getting along. As he learns to share, take turns and consider the rights of others, he can become a cooperating member of the group. He can be encouraged to respond in friendly ways and find pleasure in performing simple tasks for others. Plan experiences that will allow the child to work in small groups. Praise the child who shows kindness to others. Above all, show friendliness and kindness yourself. A four year old contines to understand best what he sees and experiences. And he is observing and absorbing the example of Christian love and concern shown by you, his teacher.

As the child develops this interest in others, he is building the foundations for his concern to share the story of Jesus with people who do not know Him. Talk with the child about children who have never heard of Jesus' love. Involve the child in a simple project, such as helping you write a letter to a missionary and drawing pictures to accompany the letter. Talking about more than one missionary is confusing to a young child. After consultation with your pastor, select one missionary your church supports. Display pictures of the missionary and his family. To encourage the child's personal interest use related pictures and objects to illustrate the kind of work the missionary does (teaching, medical, agricultural, translation, etc.); and to show the country in which he serves. Help children pray each Sunday for the missionary's needs.

THE FOUR YEAR OLD CAN LEARN ABOUT HIMSELF.

He can learn that he is a person of worth and ability. To be valued by others is not just a nice experience;

it is a vital one. A four year old can learn that he can do things for himself. He can learn that God loves him and is concerned about him as an individual. The child learns of God's love by experiencing the love of understanding adults. Demonstrate a constant, dependable love Sunday after Sunday. Remember that God made each child an individual, different from all others. Love the child for what he is right now, not for what your fond dreams hope he may become.

Before a four year old can have satisfactory relations with others, he must feel good about himself. Provide experiences in which he can succeed. To master a skill a child needs repeated opportunities at practicing that skill. For instance, by offering collage construction each Sunday of a unit, the child can increase his ability to use scissors and paste. A feeling of success is a vital first step in developing a concept of self-worth.

Have words of praise and encouragement for each child. Craig was building a house with the blocks. Because of awkward placement of blocks and excessive height his building kept falling down. Mr. Scott sat down on the floor next to him. "Craig, you certainly are building an interesting construction," he said. "I wonder if it would help to put the block on its side, like this?" Then Mr. Scott sat nearby and watched as Craig completed his house. His occasional comment allowed Craig to complete his house successfully, and to feel confident in his ability to work with blocks. "Craig, you're a fine builder! I like your work."

STOP! Before you continue, do these two things:

1 *List three ways in which you can help a child feel good about himself. Include these in your next Sunday's procedures.*

2 *Plan a visit to the sanctuary, using the guidelines suggested in this chapter. Write down what you expect the children to see and do; what special thing you want them to look for; and questions they might ask.*

CHAPTER FIVE

THE FIVE YEAR OLD

How wonderfully God has made each child! Although no two are alike, children seem to follow a prescribed pattern of growth and development. Yet, each is so influenced by his environment, heredity and other factors that he proceeds through this pattern of development at his own unique pace—different from all others.

Because of the uniqueness of each child, the teacher must become aware of his needs and abilities and ask God for wisdom to meet these needs. *But if any of you lacks wisdom, let him ask God, who gives to everyone without reserve and without faultfinding, and it will be granted him.*[1]

What is a five year old like? Use the following characteristics as a guide in planning experiences for those children with whom you work.

THE FIVE YEAR OLD IS PHYSICALLY ACTIVE.

He enjoys large muscle activities. He is rapidly developing skill in using his body, legs and arms. Although he is less restless than when he was four, he needs exercise. Provide opportunities for bodily movement. Reinforce the lesson aim with activities using large muscles such as dramatic play, finger fun and action songs that require jumping, stretching and bending. Offer block building as one of your every-Sunday learning activities. Fives need plenty of room in which to move about. Keep furnishings to a minimum.

Encourage freehand drawing with large crayons. Provide clay or salt/flour dough for the child to use.

Alternate active and quiet experiences so children are not required to sit still for long periods.

While the child's growth rate is slowing, girls are maturing more rapidly than boys in their physical development. For instance, boys who become restless during a large group activity might simply be reflecting their physical inability to sit motionless for more than a few minutes.

THE FIVE YEAR OLD LIKES TO HELP.

By helping he receives the approval and attention he needs and seeks. Helping tasks such as passing materials and picking up scraps also helps the child work off some of his excess energy. Give him responsibilities which he can perform successfully. Praise him when he completes a task. The children had just finished planting seeds at the God's Wonders table. Mr. Hardy said, "Ricky, I need you to help clean up. Will you please put these papers in the wastebasket? . . . Andy, you may put these spoons in the sink." When each child completed his task, Mr. Hardy showed his approval. "Thank you, Ricky. Thank you, Andy. You were fine helpers. Now our table is clean." While the children picked up the crayons and put away the drawing paper, Mrs. Carson sang, "Jesus was a helper, and so am I. . . ."[2] Some of the children sang along with her. When the area was clean Mrs. Carson said, "You were all fine helpers. Jesus is pleased when we help."

THE FIVE YEAR OLD'S ATTENTION SPAN IS STILL LIMITED.

He is attentive only as long as he is interested. Do not expect him to sit quietly for long periods. During Together Time provide a variety of lesson-related activities in which he can have a part; change activities frequently. Offer several Bible learning activities each Sunday. Expect the child to move from one to another.

When you tell a story, use visual resources to sustain the child's interest. Use action words such as *run, walk* or *climb.* Change the inflection of your voice to create feelings of excitement, weariness, happiness, etc. Occasionally whisper to create a quiet mood. "The wind howled. The big waves crashed against the little boat. Then, Jesus said, 'Be still!' The wind stopped howling. The waves stopped crashing (whisper) and everything was calm and still."

THE FIVE YEAR OLD'S SMALL MUSCLES
ARE UNDER BETTER CONTROL
THAN WHEN HE WAS FOUR.

He enjoys assembling construction toys; however, do not expect him to color accurately within lines. Also, cutting accurately is still difficult for some fives.

Most five year olds are learning to write (print) in public school kindergarten. Praise their accomplishments. However, be careful not to embarrass the child who is not yet able to write. Find other areas in which he can receive equal praise.

THE FIVE YEAR OLD IS CURIOUS AND EAGER TO LEARN.

He learns rapidly and asks many questions. Answer his questions simply in ways that will stimulate his own thinking. Never tell a child what he can find out for himself. Bobby was using the magnet at the God's Wonders table. "Why won't the magnet pick up this box?" he asked.

"Let's see if we can find out," answered Mrs. Collins. "Will it pick up this nail?" Together Mrs. Collins and Bobby tried to pick up various objects with the magnet. As they worked, Mrs. Collins guided Bobby's thinking until he reached the conclusion that a magnet only picks up certain kinds of metal.

A five year old still relies on his senses for most of his learning. Use objects he can see, touch, smell, taste and hear. Provide many opportunities for activities which are within his ability. Be sensitive enough to step in when help is needed, but not to interfere when the child is able to complete a task successfully.

The five year old interprets words literally; he does not understand symbolic concepts. Use words that mean exactly what they say. Avoid symbolic ideas, such as "sunbeams for Jesus," "ask Jesus into your heart," etc.

THE FIVE YEAR OLD NEEDS AFFECTION AND SECURITY.

He relies on consistent and dependable adult supervision. He finds security in knowing what is expected of him. He needs limits. He needs to know that limits set by those who love us can be *for our good always*.[3] Establish a routine with which he can become familiar. Keep materials in the same locations so the child knows where they can be found.

The child seeks affection from other children and adults. He is anxious for adult approval and wants to establish a good relationship between himself and his teacher. Give the child individual attention. Listen closely when he talks to you. Let him know with a smile, a word of praise, a hug or a pat on the shoulder that he's special to you.

The five year old enjoys working in small groups. Plan activities to be done with two to five children. Give the child considerable freedom in choosing the group in which he will work.

Five year olds are able to plan and work together on simple projects. Offer activities that allow an exchange of ideas among the children. For instance, to illustrate a Bible teaching/learning aim involving thankfulness for food, Mr. Lee suggested several children make a mural. He posted on the bulletin board a long sheet of butcher paper. Then he gave those interested food pictures torn from magazines, scissors to trim the pictures and paste. The children then completed the mural in the way they thought best. A teacher nearby guided the children's thoughts toward knowing God made our food and thanking Him for it.

Accept each child for who he is—an individual created by God. Avoid comparing him with other children. To determine his growth in any area of development, compare him with himself when he first entered your department.

STOP! Before you continue, answer these two questions:

1   *How will knowing the behavior traits typical of a five year old affect your planning and procedures?*

2   *Why is it important for you to take into account that not all children develop at the same pace?*

WHAT CAN A FIVE YEAR OLD LEARN?

Eating an elephant is an easy task when it is cut into bite-size pieces! Learning goals, like elephants, seem quite formidable until they too are "cut into bite-size pieces." To accomplish the goal of helping a child respond in love to God and the Lord Jesus, we need to proceed one step at a time. One of the beginning steps is to know what specific things the child is ready to learn at a given age.

THE FIVE YEAR OLD CAN LEARN ABOUT GOD.

He can know God made him and God loves him. He can know God desires his love; and wants him to do what is right. Use Bible stories and Bible verses to reassure the child of God's love and care. Remind him in your conversation that God wants him to *do all that is right and good.*[4] "Eric, you were very kind to share your clay with Cathy. God is glad when we are kind to our friends."

The young child can know that God is interested in his everyday experiences. Help him associate God with all that is good in his own life; his pleasant experiences, his family, his food, etc. Pamela came into Sunday school eager to tell her teacher about the picnic she had had with her family the day before. Mrs. Nelson sat down and listened attentively as Pamela told her about her happy day. When she had finished, Mrs. Nelson said, "I'm glad you had a good time, Pam. God planned for us to have happy times with our families."

THE FIVE YEAR OLD CAN KNOW THAT HE CAN TALK TO GOD.

He can begin to phrase his own simple prayers. Plan experiences throughout the morning that will provide natural opportunities for prayer. Pray simply, using words the child can understand. To help a child pray in his own words, show pictures of things familiar to him (home, family, food, church). "God helps us have our (family). Who are the ones in your family? . . . You can thank God for them." Or, let the child choose another picture of something for which he wants to thank God.

The child can know that God not only loves him, but wants him to love others. For the young child, the most effective example of God's love continues to be the loving, concerned adult. As a redeemed member of God's family, you can reflect some of the patience, kindness and forgiveness you have experienced in God's love.

THE FIVE YEAR OLD CAN LEARN ABOUT JESUS.

He can know God sent Jesus as a baby; that Jesus grew just as he is growing. He can know Jesus is a special friend and helper. To help the child learn about Jesus through stories, tell simple Bible stories within his interest. Use Bible verses and songs to reinforce learning about Jesus as a friend and helper. As the children work, you might sing songs such as, "Jesus is My Best Friend."[2]

Since most five year olds are beginning to understand family relationships they can know that Jesus is God's Son. Reinforce this learning with a picture of Jesus, lest a child understand your words to mean God's sun.

The five year old can know that Jesus is a special person who taught and showed us what God is like. He can know God wants us to live the way Jesus taught. Direct the child's thoughts to what Jesus did and said. To encourage the child to do friendly things for others, plan situations where he can put his friendliness and kindness into action.

To a young child whose world is full of phenomenal science and space achievements, the miracles of Jesus seem simply another interesting fact. As you tell stories in which Jesus helped others through a miraculous deed, emphasize Jesus' love and concern for the person who needed His love. The miracle itself was simply Jesus' way of helping. Help the child know only Jesus can help in such a wonderful way because Jesus is God's Son.

THE CHILD CAN LEARN THAT GOD WANTS EVERYONE TO LEARN ABOUT JESUS.

He can begin to show an interest in sharing stories about Jesus with other children. Generally he'll respond with enthusiasm to the idea of inviting his friends to Sunday school. Help him to know some of his love gift money helps buy Bible storybooks for other children so they can learn about Jesus.

The young child is very conscious of your feelings as you tell him about Jesus. The love for Jesus he sees you express helps determine his own feelings about Jesus.

THE FIVE YEAR OLD CAN LEARN ABOUT THE BIBLE.

He can know the Bible is a special book that tells about God and Jesus. He can know the Bible tells us ways God wants us to live. He can know the Bible is for everyone. The Bible stories in your *Leader's/Teacher's Manual* have been thoughtfully and carefully selected to reinforce the unit Bible teaching/learning aim. As you present these stories be sure the child knows they come from the Bible.

The child needs to see the Bible in use. Hold the Bible or keep it nearby as you tell the story. Underline Bible verses in red to show the child where they are located in the Bible. Keep a Bible in various areas of the room for quick use and identification of Bible words.

Each department should have a Picture Bible. To make a Picture Bible, insert the Bible story pictures from the child's Bible storybook or leaflet near the Scripture passage it illustrates. Shade the Scripture passages in red. The child will enjoy "reading" his favorite stories. Show the child how to handle the Bible and turn pages carefully.

The five year old can easily memorize simple Bible verses through repetition. Keep in mind, however, he often memorizes without understanding what the words mean. Relate the Bible verses to his everyday experiences. Use pictures and story play to illustrate and clarify meaning. Simply memorizing Bible verses is not our goal. Rather, we are concerned that a child understand and live the Bible truths.

THE FIVE YEAR OLD CAN LEARN ABOUT THE CHURCH.

He can know the church is a special place where he can come with others to learn about God and Jesus. The five year old's growing concept of the church begins with interesting and meaningful experiences planned by his teacher. These happy times encourage his love for his church.

Help the child know there is a special place for him in the church and that he is missed when he is not there. Send a card or make a phone call when the child is absent. This personal attention which takes only a few minutes of your time helps him feel loved and special.

The five year old can know there are helpers in the church. Visit the minister in his office. Arrange to visit with the church secretary. Invite the custodian to visit your department and tell how he helps in the church. Talk with the child about ways he, too, can help, such as keeping the department neat, bringing a bouquet of flowers for the interest center, etc.

The child needs to understand that the church is more than just his Sunday school room. He needs to see other parts of the church building. Plan a visit to the sanctuary. Arrange ahead of time for the organist to play a familiar song. To make it a profitable learning experience, tell the child where he is going and what he will see (big Bible on pulpit, pews, etc.). Give him something specific to look for. When you return, talk about what he saw. Take a walk around the church exterior. Point out the steeple, the cross, the big doors, etc.

The five year old can understand how some of his love gift money buys equipment and supplies to be used in the church. Provide concrete examples by using a portion of children's love gift money to buy an item, such as a box of crayons, a book or a picture for the department.

Help the child know the church is a place where we work together to help others. Plan simple missionary projects to help him understand another way his love gift money is used. Specific suggestions are given in units of your *Leader's/Teacher's Manual.*

THE FIVE YEAR OLD CAN DEVELOP LOVING ATTITUDES TOWARD OTHERS.

He can learn to respond in friendly ways; he can feel joy in doing things for others. He can become a co-operating member of the group as he shares, takes turns and considers the rights of others. Plan activities that involve working in small groups. Praise the child who shows kindness to another. Encourage an exchange of ideas by asking children to listen when one child has something to tell them.

The five year old has stepped beyond the circle of his family. In most cases he has entered kindergarten in public school. He is becoming aware of the community around him. Help him appreciate the contributions others make to his own well-being and happiness. Be sure he knows God's plan is that all people *help one another.* Mr. Anderson sat down beside David and Doug who were building a large building with blocks. "That's a fine building, boys. Can you tell me about it?" he asked.

"We're building a fire station," answered David.

Mr. Anderson and the boys talked briefly about why we need firemen. Then Mr. Anderson said, "God planned for some men to be firemen. Firemen help keep us safe."

The child's growing interest in others can lead to a concern that other boys and girls learn about Jesus. He can understand that God wants him to have a part in *teaching all nations.* Because of his age, his part is, of course, a limited one. However, he can begin by inviting his friends to Sunday school. As he understands the broader scope of missions, he can pray for his missionary friends; he can bring his love gifts so the missionary can have Bibles, pictures, medicine, food, etc. Since talk of many people and places is confusing to the young child, select one missionary (after consultation with your pastor). Learn his specific needs and decide how your department can best help him. Illustrate these needs in terms children in your department can understand. For example, if your missionary needs a church building, on a picture of a church, add a small brick figure cut from paper for each (dollar) given.

THE FIVE YEAR OLD CAN LEARN ABOUT HIMSELF.

He can grow in the knowledge that he is a person of worth and ability. Provide experiences in which he can succeed. Praise his accomplishments. Plan experiences in which he can do things for himself. Putting on wraps, using and caring for materials help the child feel independent. The thoughtful teacher will let the child do as much as possible for himself and offer assistance only when the child begins to show signs of frustration.

Jesus said, *You must love others as much as yourself.*[5] Before a child can relate well to other children, he must have a good feeling about himself—a good self-image. The feeling that he is loved, secure and has worth as an individual all help create the child's good image of himself. A teacher who knows and uses the child's name, listens when he talks and shows a sincere interest in him is saying, "I love you. You are important to me." The child finds security in feeling loved and important.

The children in your department come from different and varied backgrounds. There will be children from Christian homes where the love of God is a natural part of everyday conversation. There will be children who have never heard about God's love. There will be children who have been in Sunday school since birth and there will be those who are attending for the first time. Meet each child where he is; plan experiences through which he can learn of God's love. *Teach a child to choose the right path, and when he is older he will remain upon it.*[6]

STOP! *Before you continue, do these two things:*

1   *Plan an activity for use during Bible Learning Activity Time that will help the child learn about God as Creator. Write a brief description of the activity including materials needed and conversation you will use.*

2   *List several ways you can help children learn that Jesus is a special friend and helper. Include Scripture, songs, activities and conversation in your list. Consult your* Teacher's Manual.

CHAPTER SIX

THE NEEDS OF YOUNG CHILDREN

The young child is a person—a growing personality. He is different from every other child; he must be treated as an individual. However, each child shares certain basic needs; needs that must be met if he is to grow *in wisdom and stature, and in favour with God and man.*[1]

The young child cannot always express his needs verbally as he might when he asks for a drink of water. (What young child can turn to an adult and say, "Please make me secure"?) However, his actions might indicate that he is actually crying out to be loved or accepted. How sad if his cries are not heard! Be aware of the child's needs and sensitive to the ways in which he requests that they be met.

LOVE

The Lord said, *I have loved you with an everlasting love.*[2] A child needs love that is unconditional and ever available; a love that expresses a concern to give a child what he requires for all areas of his growth and development. A child needs to know that he matters very much to someone and that someone cares what happens to him. Sometimes a child who is misbehaving is in reality saying, "Hey! look at me. Show me that you love me!"

Help the child feel that he is loved and accepted regardless of what he does or does not do. Your actions, your smile, even your tone of voice can say "I love you." For one child a smile across the room or a friendly pat on the shoulder is enough to let him know he's important to you. For another it takes a hug or a few minutes of cuddling to let him know he's special. Help him feel he is as important as any other child in the room. Use his name often as you talk with him. Appreciate each child for himself. Sometimes the child who seems the least lovable is the one who needs love the most. Pray for that child and ask God to show love to him through you.

Offer honest praise and encouragement. Listen to the child when he speaks to you. Bend down to his eye level; show a genuine interest in what he has to tell you. Send a card or telephone a child who is absent on Sunday morning. Take a few extra minutes occasionally to send a note to a child who attends every Sunday. Let him know how happy you are to see him each week.

A child's feeling that he is loved is the foundation on which he builds love toward others. A child learns to love by being loved. As he has continuing opportunities to love and to be loved, love will become part of his pattern of living.

A child understands God's love as he experiences love from understanding adults. He needs to see God's love reflected in the attitudes and actions of his teachers and other adults who love God. *You are Christ's epistle . . . written not with ink but with the Spirit of the living God; not on tablets of stone but on human tablets of the heart.*[3]

SECURITY

The young child is "stepping out." He is taking those important first steps toward independence and finding himself as a person. When he is five (or younger if he attends nursery school) he usually begins public school kindergarten and moves beyond the circle of his family. He needs to know that while he may reach out for new and exciting adventures, he can depend upon his own world to remain familiar and comforting.

Knowing and feeling he is loved is essential to a child's feeling of security. Show him through your actions that you love him. Show him that he is important to you because he is himself, not because of the way he compares with other children. It is through experiencing your love that the child begins to understand God's love. When he feels secure and comfortable in your love, he will begin to feel secure in God's love.

The child finds security in familiar surroundings and procedures. Plan a program that follows the same general routine every Sunday. (Of course, there will be times when one part of the schedule might be shortened or lengthened according to children's interests.) Supply basic equipment that will be available to the child each Sunday. He enjoys using the same toys again and again. Tell favorite stories often. Repeat familiar songs and finger fun activities over and over. The young child also finds security in knowing his teacher will be in Sunday school each week. The teacher who is faithful in her attendance and in her loving care of the children entrusted to her is expressing God's love in a way these little ones can understand.

The child finds security in limits. He needs to know what is expected of him, what he can and cannot do in the department room. Establishing limits to insure children's physical safety is your first consideration. (No child leaves the room alone, etc.) Then set limits for the appropriate use of equipment and material. For instance, puzzle pieces must be kept on table; blocks remain in building area; home living area equipment must not be stepped on. Allow as much freedom as possible within these limits. Be consistent. Avoid forbidding certain behavior at one time but allowing the same behavior later under the same circumstances. When you remind a child of limits, phrase your words positively. "We keep puzzle pieces on the table," rather than, "Don't carry away the puzzle pieces."

ACCEPTANCE

A child needs to feel that he is acceptable just the way he is; that he is accepted all the time regardless of the way he looks, the clothes he wears or whether he is "good" or "bad." A child who feels loved and accepted for himself—not for what he does—will gain self-confidence and feel valued as a person. If he feels he must earn acceptance he may feel insecure and unworthy. His rebellious or aggressive behavior might be a means of attracting attention to his need for acceptance.

When a child exhibits feelings of anger or unfriendliness, accept the child even though you do not approve of his behavior. Approval and acceptance are two different things. Acceptance means recognizing his feelings without blaming. It does not mean permitting the child to demonstrate unacceptable behavior. The limits you set must be enforced; and the welfare of the other children considered.

For instance, when Scott, with a scowl on his face, comes to the block building area and deliberately kicks over Sharon's construction, an initial reaction might be to say, "Stop that! You're a bad boy!" However, the thoughtful teacher might put her hand on Scott's shoulder, guide him away from the area and say, "Scott, you are feeling angry right now. But I cannot let you knock down Sharon's building." The teacher recognizes Scott's angry feelings. She does not label his actions. "We will need to help Sharon build her garage again." If Scott seems disinterested, the teacher might guide him to a table activity where he could work individually, yet with an understanding adult nearby. "Here is some dough to work with. Mr. Hardy has popsicle sticks for you to cut the dough." The teacher returns to the block building area to clarify Scott's actions and help restore Sharon's building. "Scott was feeling angry. I am sorry he kicked over your building. When he feels happy again, he can work with his friends."

The child who feels loved and accepted by adults will find it easier to feel accepted by God. Help the child know that he is acceptable to God at all times. Avoid giving the impression that God will not love him if he is naughty. God's love is a free, unconditional gift. God never withholds love to secure obedience.

In order to accept a child you must first understand

him. How well do you know each child in your class? Observe him thoughtfully, arrange visits to his home, listen to his chatter, as he plays, talk and work with him on an individual basis. Learning to understand each child will provide a sound basis for an understanding acceptance of him.

SELF-CONTROL

A child is not born with the ability to control his own actions. He must develop self-control with the careful guidance of adults he trusts. Developing this self-control does not happen overnight. It takes time. A child first needs to know what adults expect of him. After he has tested these limits and found them to be consistent, he can begin to develop his own system of self-control. By adhering to a well organized routine and enforcing a few rules of conduct, adults encourage the child in his efforts to be responsible for his own actions.

To develop self-control, the child also needs consistent, positive guidance. He needs a balance between rigid authority and total permissiveness. He needs limits, but with freedom to move about within those limits. When a child receives thoughtful and careful guidance, a learning process takes place and the child becomes responsible for his own behavior. From this responsibility grows self-control—discipline from within.

INDEPENDENCE

The young child's plea "Let me do it!" is evidence of his first steps toward independence. He is attempting to discover his own abilities. He needs to know he can do things on his own, but with the assurance there is an understanding teacher nearby on whom he can depend if he needs assistance.

Careful, thoughtful guidance will help the child toward attaining independence. Give him freedom in choosing materials and activities. Free choice requires that materials be readily accessible. Arrange materials so the child knows where they are, can reach materials without asking for assistance and return them when he is through. Display materials so they are seeable, reachable and returnable. Provide hooks or a coat rack that are low enough to allow the child to hang up his own wraps.

In order to grow in independence, the child must be allowed to assume responsibility when he shows he is ready. Give the child as much independence as he can handle. Encourage his efforts and praise his accomplishments. Because children's skills vary, you need to know the ability of each child in your group. Select tasks of which he is capable. Let him do as much as possible on his own. When it is necessay to step in, give suggestions that will enable the child to experience success.

For example, "Do you think the puzzle piece will fit if you turn it around?" or "It might be easier for you to hang up your coat if I hold the hanger very still."

Allowing a child to do things for himself and others often requires extra time. Plan your schedule so as to avoid the words, "Hurry up." Rushing young children almost always results in frustration for all concerned.

RECOGNITION OF WORTH

Each young child needs to be assured of his own, unique, place in the world of people. He needs assurance of his worth as an individual. What a child believes about himself affects everything he does, even what he sees and hears. Helping a child feel good about himself is not building conceit. It is rather enabling him to try, to be creative, to make use of his world.

Consider how important the individual is to God. Not one sparrow can fall to the ground without God's knowledge and yet each of us is worth more to God than a sparrow. God is so aware of us as individuals that even the hairs on our heads have all been numbered.[4] When a child feels he has worth in the eyes of his parents and teachers, he will be better able to understand that he has worth in the eyes of God.

A child's recognition of his own worth depends largely on his experiences of love, security and acceptance expressed by adults. How can a child feel wanted unless someone wants him? How can the child feel acceptable unless someone accepts him? When he feels secure in the love and acceptance of adults around him, he can begin to feel good about himself. When he realizes that he has certain rights and dignity as an individual, he can more readily recognize the rights and dignity of others.

Treat the child with respect. Sometimes adults neglect to show a young child respect because they forget that he too is a person. He deserves to be heard. Listen attentively when he talks to you. Use his name often in your conversation with him. Never shame him; avoid labeling him a "bad boy" or "a baby." Extend to him the common courtesies you would show his parents. Hearing "please", "thank you", "excuse me" or "I'm sorry" will help the child feel he is a worthwhile person.

PROTECTION

The value of each child in your care is beyond price! And each child needs protection. He needs to know he will be kept from harm. He needs to know he will have help when he must face strange, unknown and frightening situations.

Protect the child from physical harm. To prevent accidents before they happen, be alert for potentially dangerous situations. Check toys and other equipment regularly for sharp points and edges. Be sure furniture is sturdy, free from splinters and in good repair. Be alert for a child who does not feel well. If a child becomes ill, send for his parents. Help parents be aware of the necessity for enforcing certain health and safety regulations that protect all children. Help them understand the importance of keeping a child at home if he appears ill.

Protect the child from emotional harm. Be aware of his emotional needs and how you can meet them. Understand the child's fears and help him cope with them in a realistic way. Never ridicule or shame him. Help the child feel secure in your love and protection. Reassure him of God's loving care.

Understanding the young child is no easy task!

Sometimes his behavior can be frustrating. Sometimes we make errors in interpreting his actions. Nevertheless every young child needs adults who are willing to attempt to understand the way he feels and why he acts as he does. He needs adults who will love him enough to give him what his behavior shows he needs. Then they are expressing God's love to him in ways within his understanding.

STOP! Before you continue, do these two things:

1 *Name several ways you can help a child feel he is loved. Think in terms of specific children.*

2 *List several children in your department whom you feel need additional experience toward developing independence. What opportunities can you offer next Sunday to encourage them to do things for themselves?*

CHAPTER 1

1. *Little Ones Sing,* Revised Edition, (Glendale, Calif.: G/L Publications, 1972).
2. See 1 Peter 5:7, *King James Version.*
3. Ecclesiastes 3:11, *KJV*

CHAPTER 2

1. Ecclesiastes 3:1, *The Berkeley Version in Modern English,* (Grand Rapids: Zondervan Publishing House, 1959) Used by permission.
2. *Little Ones Sing,* Revised
3. Haystead, Wesley, *Ways to Plan and Organize Your Sunday School,* Early Childhood—Birth to 5 years, (Glendale, Calif.: G/L Publications, 1971).

CHAPTER 3

1. *Little Ones Sing,* Revised
2. Luke 19:1-10
3. John 15:12, *KJV*
4. Matthew 19:19, *Berkeley*

CHAPTER 4

1. Luke 2:52, *The Living Bible,* Paraphrased (Wheaton, Ill.: Tyndale House, Publishers, 1971).
2. Ephesians 4:15, *Living Bible*

CHAPTER 5

1. James 1:5, *Berkeley*
2. *Little Ones Sing,* Revised
3. Deuteronomy 6:24, *KJV*
4. Deuteronomy 6:18, *Berkeley*
5. Mark 12:31, *Living Bible*
6. Proverbs 22:6, *Living Bible*

CHAPTER 6

1. Luke 2:52, *KJV*
2. Jeremiah 31:3, *Berkeley*
3. 2 Corinthians 3:3, *Berkeley*
4. See Matthew 10:30,31.

PART II

LEARNING

THANK YOU
FOR PRET

CHAPTER SEVEN

WHAT IS LEARNING?

Early childhood education is an area of interest and concern that is exploding with excitement. Young children are in the world's educational spotlight. This feeling of excitement and the focus of attention on young children is the result of recent scientific data indicating the importance of what and how a child is capable of learning in his first years.

Noted educator B.S. Bloom quotes research that indicates a child's mature intelligence (his ability to understand and relate. . .) usually reaches 50% of its development by the time he is four years old. Also, Bloom explains, the child's basic personality characteristics formed in these early years will probably never change. This information would cause us to rephrase the biblical statement of Proverbs even more strongly to read, ". . . and when he is old he will not *be able* to depart from it."

The church, then, must give immediate attention to the important task of providing the very best quality of Christian education for its young children. As Christian educators formulating a learning program for these years of early childhood, we begin with a long-range goal: to help the child learn Bible truths so that at God's appointed time and with the enabling power of the Holy Spirit, the child will express faith in the Lord Jesus Christ as Saviour and will become a regenerated, a born again member in God's family of believers.

We believe that this born again experience is so essential to every person that we feel a sense of great urgency about helping the child in his first years to begin learning Bible truths. Let us be sure, first of all, that we understand what we mean when we say *learn* Bible truths. For our definition, the term *learning* is the key to the why, what and how of our teaching!

Learning is a process involving a variety of experiences by which a person gains information, understanding and skills which have a lasting effect on his behavior. As a child grows and develops, he accumulates factual information and acquires attitudes about many things. When he puts together his information and attitudes in ways that affect his behavior, we say the child has learned. The information and attitudes of these early years are so important in determining behavior patterns that we dare not neglect our goal of helping the little child learn simple Bible truths, even before he may understand what it means to be a born again member of God's redeemed family of believers.

Furthermore, this learning involves our helping him discover ways he may behave in loving response and obedience to the Lord and to His Word. This process begins even before the child may comprehend what it means to be a born again member of God's redeemed family of believers. For this is the nurture and training we, who are members of the Body, are reminded to provide children entrusted to our care. This is the beginning of learning Bible truths *that make you wise to accept God's salvation by trusting in Christ Jesus. The whole Bible was given to us by inspiration from God and is useful to teach us what is true and to make us realize what is wrong in our lives; it straightens us out and helps us do what is right. It is God's way of making us well prepared at every point, fully equipped to do good to everyone.*[2]

A second reason for helping a child to know, to understand and to respond to Bible truths is that we may help to prepare the soil into which the seed of the Word may take root and grow at God's appointed time. Statistics indicate that most conversions among children take place between ages of ten and twelve. However, the child who attends Sunday School during his early years—and particularly those from warm Christian homes—soon believes that Jesus loves him and is his friend; that Jesus wants his love in return.

A third reason for helping a little child learn Bible truths is to show him ways of thinking, acting and behaving in accord with the instructions from God's Word. By observing the attitudes and actions of adults around him, the little child begins to recognize sharing, helping, kindness and other expressions of love as patterns of life for those who love the Lord Jesus.

A fourth reason for guiding the young child to know Bible truths is so that he might have a biblical awareness of the world in which he lives. By this we mean that we want him to feel that his own life and his world of people and experiences are all a part of God's loving plan and care. If the young child can early believe in and count on God's unconditional love for him as a person of great worth, he can begin to cope with the experiences of living in today's world in the security of His unchanging love. And this confidence in God's dependability is a reflection of one's learning that God can be trusted.

Fifth, we want the child to be receptive toward, to be interested in, to develop positive attitudes toward God's Word. We want the child to understand that what God has to say in the Bible is of primary importance to all of life. And the young child—in his impressionable and open mind and heart—*can* know, understand and respond in love to God's love and concern for him as he hears again and again the truths of the living Word.

We cannot assume that helping a child learn Bible truths by encouraging him to make his behavior conform to biblical principles will make him become a Christian. We do believe, however, that a child's becoming familiar with what God's Word teaches and his being guided to practice acceptable behavior instructed by God for those in the family of believers is important preparation of the soil to receive the Word of life. And this preparation is the "train up a child" principle in which God directs us for the Christian nurture of those of whom Jesus said, *"Let the little children come to Me, and don't prevent them. For*

such is the Kingdom of Heaven. For I tell you that
heaven their angels have constant access to My Fa-
ther."[3]

THE LEARNING PROCESS

To guide young children in learning Bible truths effectively, leaders and teachers need to consider two
important aspects of the learning process: What are
some of the basic conditions that affect a child's
learning and what are some of the ways a child
learns.

CONDITIONS FOR LEARNING

A young child learns best when he is READY to learn.
No amount of a mother's desire for her child to walk
will make his muscles mature enough for walking. He
must be ready! This readiness to learn includes his
interest and desire as well as his maturity. Trying to
push a child into learning something for which he is
not ready causes frustration that may hinder his later
learning. Too many failures and the child is reluctant
to try again.

Teachers who understand that a child is ready to
learn provide materials and equipment that are attractive, inviting and within his general capability. For instance, one teacher knew the little ones in her department would have difficulty in using doll clothes with
tiny snaps and small neck openings. So she made doll
clothes that open down the front, generous enough in
size to wrap around easily.

A child learns best when he experiences success in
the learning. A wise teacher plans activities and experiences on the child's readiness level so he will be
able to feel the joy of accomplishment. For instance,
she provides puzzles that a young child can assemble
with ease; art work he can do without too much difficulty, and blocks he can easily manage. A child will
most likely want to return to Sunday school if his experiences there have been pleasant and successful.

Another important ingredient in helping a child experience achievement is the teacher's honest praise
and approval. A smile, a hug or a word of commenda-

ion helps a child feel satisfaction. These good feelings give the child encouragement to continue his learning experiences. An understanding teacher is ready with expressions such as, "I like the way Tom builds with blocks!" "Sharon really knows about puzzles!" "My, what a fine helper Jerry is!" "Just look at Beth's interesting work!"

A child's total environment—his physical surroundings and the adults with whom he has contact—affect his learning. A pleasant and comfortable room, equipped with appropriate age-level materials make for easier learning. Positive relationships with mature Christian adults, whose attitudes and actions reflect God's love, contribute greatly to the way a child feels about learning.

Firsthand experiences are the hard core of learning for young children. "Let ME do it!" is their familiar plea. A child learns by doing and most always, doing is playing. His play is his work. In the adult world a distinction is often made between work and play. Not so in the world of young children! Play is his full time occupation, just as important at this time in his life as his father's work or his mother's home management.

A child's play experiences should involve as many of his five senses as possible. He needs to participate directly in seeing, hearing, touching, smelling, tasting. "Let me see it!" really means "Let me feel it. Let me examine it!" Through his senses the child learns of God's world and the people in it. As you plan learning activities for young children, ask yourself, "How many senses will they use as they participate in these experiences?"

"Let's do it again!" is another favorite expression of young children. If a child feels happy and satisfied with his learning experience, he will want to repeat it. Repetition is a necessary (and natural) part of a child's learning. Songs and stories become favorites only when they are enjoyed over and over. Children need opportunities to repeat their learning in a variety of ways. How can a child be kind, helpful and loving unless he has many different opportunities to practice these concepts through firsthand experiences that have meaning for him in everyday life? For example a teacher needs to plan learning experiences that may help a child solve problems, learn to get along with other children, stimulate his language growth and help him understand the role of each family member. The repetition of these firsthand experiences strengthens habits, attitudes, knowledge and understanding that reflect Christian values.

USING YOUR CURRICULUM

The Early Childhood courses of G/L Curriculum have been especially developed to help you teach Bible truths in the ways young children learn best. The material in each *Leader's/Teacher's Manual* is divided into three units which cover approximately a three month period of time. Each of these three units consists of four or five lessons, all with a similar purpose. This unit plan for grouping the lessons will help you think of each unit more as one continuing lesson rather than as a series of four or five isolated lessons.

Why do we divide the material into units? Because a young child needs time to grow with an idea, to form attitudes. He needs much repetition—an essential for his learning. Also, teachers need time to work through the material slowly in accordance with the child's own pattern of growth. At the beginning of each unit is the unit objective. It tells what you want the child to know, and what you trust his response will be. It sums up the kind of learning that should go on in your room. The Bible teaching/learning aim stated at the beginning of each lesson reflects in detail a similarity of purpose to the unit objective.

USING YOUR BIBLE TEACHING/LEARNING AIMS

This aim tells what we want the child to learn as a result of the lesson presentation(s). Aims are usually stated in three parts: what the child can *know* (facts, information); what a child may *feel* (his attitudes) and in what ways a child might *respond* (things he might do as a result of what he knows and feels). For example, the lesson Bible teaching/learning aim for "God Made Our World" reads: To help the child KNOW

God made all things; to FEEL that God lovingly planned this world for him, to RESPOND by recognizing and naming things God made; and by thanking God for these things.

Notice that these aims are stated in terms of what the *child,* not the teacher, is to do. The role of the teacher is to help the child know specific information and acquire attitudes so that the child might respond in ways that show a change in his behavior. These responses to Bible truths during the years of early childhood, seem to appear small. Nevertheless, they are significant because they are an actual beginning toward accomplishing our long-range goal of the child's acceptance of God's love through faith.

Begin your preparation by reading the Bible teaching/learning aim at the beginning of your lesson; also read the current unit aim. Ask yourself, "What experiences will help the child accomplish this aim?" Then carefully consider the Bible learning materials suggested in each lesson. Select the activities for which you believe your children are ready. Also consider your space, personnel and equipment.

STOP! Before you continue, do these two things:

1 *List the reasons you feel are most important for helping young children learn Bible truths.*
2 *Make plans to carefully observe several children in your department for four Sundays. Jot down your observations as suggested on the chart.*

NAME	ACTIVITY	WHAT WAS HIS RESPONSE	WHY
Sharon	Puzzle	Completed two puzzles by herself; seemed quite pleased with herself.	Puzzles were within her ability to complete.
Jeffrey	Group Time	Restless, inattentive	Distracted by another child; room seemed overly warm and stuffy.

Use your observations to help you determine ways to improve the teaching/learning opportunities in your department.

CHAPTER EIGHT

THE TEACHER

Let's talk about you, the one who guides young children. You may be called a leader, teacher, assistant, or helper. Whatever your title, you have a part in expressing God's love to a child. The church of Jesus Christ has entrusted you to help little ones come to Him. In accepting this responsibility, you have been called as surely as Moses was called that day at the burning bush—though possibly not as dramatically.

If you have ever doubted your qualifications to guide little ones you are not alone. When Moses heard God's call, his response was, *"I'm not the man for a job like that! . . . The people won't believe me. . . . I'm not a good speaker."*[1]

God's response to Moses was the same as it is to you today. *"I will certainly be with you. . . . I will help you to speak well. I will tell you what to do."*[2]

What are some of the qualities one who guides young children needs to possess or cultivate? First he is a *growing* person. Continuing growth in all areas of Christian life is of primary importance. This growth comes through regularly attending church, studying God's Word as well as current materials concerning young children, and fellowshiping with other Christians. When your spiritual life is growing and maturing you will be more responsive to God's love and to the leading of the Holy Spirit.

Prayer should be a regular, meaningful part of your life. Pray for your friends and community as well as for your own personal needs. Pray by name for each child in your class. Know his needs so your prayers can be specific. Pray for guidance in your lesson preparation; ask the Lord to help you make your teaching relevant as well as interesting to young children.

Those who guide young children must be *teachable*. When you sense your high calling from God, you will want to fulfill your commitment in the best possible way. Be willing to learn new and better ways to do your job. Keep abreast of today's educational trends by reading and studying current publications. Be open to the suggestions of others. Attend workshops geared to the age level with which you work. Visit other Sunday schools as well as weekday nursery schools and kindergartens.

To help make what you are teaching relevant to the needs of the children, be *flexible*. It might mean changing your method of presentation right in the middle of a lesson. For instance, Mrs. Walker was talking with five year olds about God's loving care. She was showing pictures of various places children might go, such as the market, the church, the park, or the beach. She wanted the children to feel God cares for them no matter where they are. Her conversation was interrupted by Ronnie's loud question, "What's that bird out the window doing?" Immediately, the children forgot Mrs. Walker's words and her pictures as they turned to the window to watch a bird carrying nesting materials into an outdoor light fixture.

"Let's tiptoe to the window and find out," Mrs. Walker suggested. As the children quietly watched the bird, Mrs. Walker was able to tell of ways God cares for the birds and how God cares for each child. As the children continued watching, Mrs. Walker sang softly, "God takes care of the little birds. He cares for them so tenderly. And if He takes care of the little birds, I know He will take care of me."

One who guides young children must be able to change his role according to the situation and needs of the children. At one moment you might be a question-answerer. At another moment a comforter, an arbitrator, a setter of limits or a storyteller. At times, you might be two or three different people at once.

To be flexible, one must be well prepared. Mrs. Walker was able to use Ronnie's interruption to continue and reinforce the concept of God's loving care because she was well enough prepared not to be tied to her planned picture presentation. She had learned a variety of songs; at a moment's notice she could choose one to fit the situation.

Those who guide young children must also be flexible in a physical way. It is important for you to be at the child's eye level when speaking or listening to him. Sit on low chairs or on the floor. Participate in action games, block building and other floor activities. Stooping, bending, kneeling, stretching and reaching are all part of working with young children. Wear low-heeled shoes and comfortable clothing that does not readily show soil. Women teachers need to remove their hats while working with the children. (One youngster thought that since his teacher kept on her hat, she would be leaving momentarily!)

The one who guides young children is a person who *cares.* He recognizes the reality of Christ in his own life and cares enough to want to share it with others. He becomes excited when he sees a child discover the reality of God's love or show loving concern for another.

Express your concern by loving and accepting each child. Often we reserve our concern for times of distress or trouble. Genuine love reaches out into all situations, the pleasant as well as the unpleasant. Understand the individual differences in children; become aware of the needs and potential of each child. Share the child's feeling of wonder and discovery.

Because you care, always present a neat, well-groomed personal appearance. Use a soft, pleasing voice and have a ready smile.

The direction in which you guide children's learning experiences is of utmost importance. The unit and lesson Bible teaching/learning aims stated in your *Leader's/Teacher's Manual* serve to direct thoughts, conversation and activities toward a specific objective. Each lesson's suggested activities, stories, etc. are planned to help accomplish that lesson's aim.

Study the lesson material; thoroughly prepare for that part of the program which is your responsibility.

Your role is also to *stimulate* *learning* and to provide an environment for learning. Keep the room attractive and make materials available for the children. Create an atmosphere in which children can have pleasant learning experiences. Select from the activities listed in your *Leader's/Teacher's Manual* those that you feel best relate the Bible teaching/learning aim to the young child's interest and needs. *A wise teacher makes learning a joy.*[4]

Because of their individual needs, interest and varying abilities, children require a variety of learning experiences. Plan several activities from which a child may choose. Activities that involve the child in listening, experimenting, and discovering encourage him to find answers for himself. Give the child encouragement to try a new puzzle; recognize his success.

You also serve children as a *guide.* To some it might seem much easier to simply tell young children all we think they should know. However, child specialists have discovered that children learn far more through firsthand experiences than they do from sit-still-and-listen situations. Your role is to plan and guide children in learning experiences whereby they can discover, create and accomplish things for themselves.

Those who guide young children are *listeners.* The child's words and actions are clues to his needs and understanding. Listen carefully to the child's conversation as he plays; watch his reactions to certain situations. An alert teacher can determine what concepts need clarifying and which aims need reinforcing. Most important, careful listening can help determine the needs of individual children.

Some people call guiding young children an opportunity. Others call it a challenge. The Bible calls it a gift.

STOP! *Before you continue:*

Divide a piece of paper into two columns. List your strengths as a teacher in one column and your weaknesses in another. Write down ways to improve your weaknesses.

FOOTNOTES

PART II

CHAPTER 7

1. John 1:12,13, *The Living Bible,* Paraphrased (Wheaton, Ill.: Tyndale House, Publishers, 1971).
2. 2 Timothy 3:15-17, *Living Bible*
3. Matthew 19:14 and 18:10, *Living Bible*

CHAPTER 8

1. Exodus 4:10, *Living Bible*
2. Exodus 4:12,15, *Living Bible*
3. *Little Ones Sing, Revised Edition*, (Glendale, Calif.: G/L. Publications, 1972).
4. Proverbs 15:2, *Living Bible*

PART III

LEARNING METHODS

When a child steps into your Sunday school room he arrives ready to learn. The Lord Himself has determined how a child learns. He has marvelously equipped each child with five senses. Through seeing, hearing, touching, smelling and tasting, the little ones learn of the world and people about them. Their senses enable them to *be doers of the word and not hearers only.*[1]

Bible Learning Activities (Step 1 in each lesson of your *Leader's/Teacher's Manual*) add doing to what a child is hearing and seeing throughout the morning. The activities involve the child in his home-centered world of playing out familiar experiences. Touching, smelling, tasting and experimenting at the God's Wonders table help the child relate *all things were made by Him*[2] to what he is seeing and doing. Becoming a member of the "family" at the home living area helps him better understand the meaning of *children, obey your parents.*[3] Sharing materials during an art activity gives meaning to the verse *share with others.*[4]

Bible Learning Activities give the adult assigned to each activity an opportunity to discover what is a child's level of understanding, what the child already knows about Bible truths and what misunderstandings he might have. This knowledge helps the teacher plan effectively to meet the needs of the individual child.

A young child learns through relationships. During Bible Learning Activities the teacher can work with the child on a one-to-one or one-to-two or three relationship. It is a time when the child gets to know the teacher and the teacher gets to know the child. Understanding comes through these shared experiences.

The following pages list a variety of Bible Learning Activities, and ways to incorporate specific Bible teaching/learning aims into these activities. Your *Leader's/Teacher's Manual* (Step 1 in each lesson) contains detailed suggestions for relating each lesson's aim to the child's experiences.

CHAPTER NINE

BLOCK BUILDING

Provide opportunities for block building during Bible Learning Activities (Sunday School) and Choosing Time (Church Time).

Blocks are important learning tools for all young children. The use of blocks helps a child develop physically, mentally, socially, and spiritually. Building with blocks allows him to work alone, parallel with another child or in cooperation with others in a small group. Lifting and carrying blocks helps satisfy his need for large muscle activity. Block building helps him to develop his own ideas and to make decisions. A child's imagination allows his blocks to become a car, a train, a house or a fire station. He also learns responsibility in caring for building materials.

When the child works in small groups, block building provides him with opportunities for cooperation and sharing. He learns to respect the rights and ideas of others. He has opportunities for problem solving and decision making. Block building provides firsthand experiences in practicing Christian concepts, such as sharing, helping, taking turns and exercising self-control.

Through block building the child can develop a variety of mathematical concepts. He matches, arranges and measures. He works with sizes and shapes through his sense of touch as well as sight. When he counts he deals with numbers to decide how many blocks he will need for his wall or train. He begins to learn concepts, such as many, few, more than, less than, etc. Blocks provide endless opportunities for the creation of different shapes and forms.

Block building provides the teacher, assigned to that area, opportunities to relate the lesson's Bible teaching/learning aim to the child's interests and activities. At the block area she can occasionally initiate building projects to help children become familiar with Bible-time life. For instance, on a Sunday when a well will be mentioned in the Bible story, the teacher shows a picture of a Bible-time well, guides children in building one from blocks and pretending to draw water from it. She familiarizes them with the idea of a well, so when they hear it mentioned in the story later in the morning, they can listen with understanding.

The child's use of blocks and other materials depends upon his maturity, his familiarity with the materials and his previous experiences. Expect a two year old to hold a block or carry one around with him. He may pile one block on top of another and knock them down. Occasionally he may use large hollow blocks as steps or place them end to end so he can walk on them. He is learning how blocks feel and what he can do with them.

A three year old often uses several blocks at a time. He may stack them merely for the pleasure of stacking or he may attach a name to what he is building. The pile of blocks becomes whatever the child names it, changing its identity from moment to moment.

The four year old and five year old child is becoming adept at using blocks. He is beginning to plan what he will build and how he will build it. He uses his imagination as he becomes involved in playing out an event with his construction. He enjoys using accessory toys such as boats and trucks in his block building. The five year old is beginning to put realism into his work. His work may take on the shape of a building with walls, doors, windows and a roof. He can be encouraged to build more realistically through suggestions, such as "What do you need in your building so the people can get inside?"

MATERIALS[1]

Blocks   The most commonly used blocks are wooden unit blocks and large, hollow wooden blocks. Cardboard blocks are also available from educational supply firms or mail order houses. Cardboard blocks are lightweight and easy for a two year old to manage. Wooden blocks are durable; they are available in a variety of shapes and sizes that encourage creative building. When wooden blocks show signs of wear they can be sanded and refinished. They will last many years and are worth the investment.

Blocks can also be made from empty milk cartons and cardboard boxes.[1] These cartons and boxes may be covered with a woodgrained adhesive-backed paper.

Accessory toys   The value of block building is enhanced for the threes, fours, and fives by a variety of accessory toys which encourage dramatic play. These include transportation toys, such as cars, trucks, airplanes and trains. They should be well made and durable. Wooden wheeled toys are a wise investment. Avoid inexpensive, stamped metal toys that break easily or have sharp edges.

Other accessory toys include furniture and stand-up figures of people, animals and trees. These items can be purchased or made.[1] Pieces of corrugated cardboard, 12″ by 12″, encourage the building of ramps, roofs, etc.

Fives and some fours enjoy using signs ("Airport," "Gas Station," "Church," etc.) in dramatic play. Signs should be printed in manuscript writing. The most frequently used signs should be stored in a file box near the block area. Keep a felt tip pen and large index cards handy to make new signs.

Pictures   Occasionally, a lesson in your *Leader's/ Teacher's Manual* will suggest the use of pictures to encourage children to build a specific object. Be alert for large, colorful pictures of boats, bridges, airplanes, etc., to add to your picture file.

PROCEDURE

Blocks and accessory toys that are neatly arranged

on low, open shelves invite the young child to build. The building area should be out of traffic paths to help children and adults avoid knocking down buildings or falling over blocks.

The child should be free to build what he wishes. However, a teacher is nearby to offer guidance when needed. The teacher should step in, to:

- Guide the child's thinking with appropriate comments toward the lesson's Bible teaching/learning aim. (See Step 1 in each lesson for specific conversation suggestions.)
- Redirect activity when others in the room are being disturbed by too much noise or when play has lost its purpose.
- Protect the rights and safety of children.
- Help a child who is becoming frustrated in his attempts to use blocks.

Be alert for opportunities to praise and encourage children. "Tom, you are building a strong building," ... "Jane, you are a kind helper. Our Bible tells us to *help one another* . . ." Help a timid child participate by suggesting a specific way for him to become involved. For example, "Danny, here is a place for the driver to sit. You can be our driver and drive us to church."

To help children become acquainted with a lesson-related object or concept, your *Leader's/Teacher's Manual* will sometimes suggest building a specific item. Use pictures and conversation to encourage the child's participation. "I'd like to sail in a boat like this one. . . . Let's make a boat with our blocks. . . . Pete, I need you to help with the boat." Usually, your enthusiasm will draw children into the activity. However, if they want to build something else, avoid insisting they carry out your suggestion.

Putting away blocks and accessory toys usually takes more time than other activities. Warn the children in advance that it's almost clean-up time. Stack like-sized blocks together. Pieces of woodgrained adhesive-backed paper cut the shape of the blocks and attached to shelves will mark the place where each size block should be stored.

BIBLE TEACHING/LEARNING OPPORTUNITIES

How can the teacher use block building to relate the lesson aim and Bible Thoughts to a child's interest and experience? A teacher's conversation with the young builders offers endless opportunities to help children know and do what God's Word says.

When your Bible teaching/learning aim involves SHARING, use these ideas and Bible Thoughts in your conversation:

"Lisa, you are kind to share your trucks with Kim. Our Bible says to *share what you have with others.*" During Together Time, comment on specific acts of sharing you have observed. "Billy was a kind friend in the block area today. Billy shared his blocks with Eddie. Billy knows that sharing is a way to show love."

Remember, sharing is a new word and a new idea for most twos and threes. Define its meaning in words and actions little ones can understand. "Pam has many blocks. Danny doesn't have any. Pam can let Danny use some of her blocks. That's sharing. . . . Thank you, Pam, for sharing."

Bible Thoughts for your conversation:

Share what you have with others. Hebrews 13:16

Love one another. I John 4:7

Do that which is right and good. Deuteronomy 6:18

KINDNESS

As children work with blocks identify specific acts of kindness as the way of acceptable behavior. (Simply telling a child he is a "good boy" gives him no clue as to what he did to deserve your praise.) Use Bible Thoughts naturally in your conversation. "Jack, you were kind to your friend. You were kind to help Ann carry that heavy block. Our Bible tells us to *be kind to one another*. Jesus was kind to His friends, too."

Bible Thoughts for your conversation:

Be kind toward one another. Ephesians 4:32

Treat everyone with kindness. Galatians 6:10

A friend loves at all times.   Proverbs 17:17

HELPING

There are many opportunities for the child to put God's Word into action by helping in the block area. He can carry blocks, help another child with his building and help clean up. Call attention to the child who is helpful. "Ruth is a fine helper. Thank you for putting the cars on the shelf, Ruth. . . . God is happy that *we are helpers*. . . . Mike is helping Tim with his wall. . . . Our Bible tells us to *love one another*. Helping is a good way to show love."

Clean-up time offers an ideal opportunity for a child to have firsthand experience in helping. "Our room looks very nice because we all helped put the blocks away. . . . Our Bible reminds us that *we are helpers*. . . . Keith used his strong arms to help put away the big blocks."

Bible Thoughts for your conversation:

We . . . are helpers. 2 Corinthians 1:24

I will help. 2 Samuel 10:11

[With] love, [help] one another. Galatians 5:13

CREATION

In your natural conversation help children know they use the hands, arms and legs God made when they build. A four year old and a five year old child can go a step farther and know God made their minds to think about what to build. Children can also know that God made the trees from which we get wood to make blocks. "Brian, you are using the strong arms God made to carry that big block. . . . We use our hands when we build. Who made our hands? *All things were made by God*. Cindy, what are the blocks made of? Where do we get wood to make blocks? We get wood from trees. *God is good* to make trees."

Bible Thoughts for your conversation:

[God] made everything. Ecclesiastes 3:11

God is good. Psalm 73:1

All things were made by [God]. John 1:3

God . . . made the world and everything in it.
Acts 17:24

[God] made . . . the stars. Genesis 1:16

THANKFULNESS

Help children respond in thankfulness to God for hands with which to build; for the blocks and toys they use; for friends with whom they work and have happy times. "I'm glad God made our hands so we can build with blocks. We can thank God for our hands. . . . Let's tell God thank you for our blocks and toys. *It is good to give thanks to the Lord.* . . . Kris and Kevin worked together to build a big fire station. God planned for us to have friends so we can have happy times together. We can tell God 'thank you' for our friends." If children seem receptive, pray a brief prayer of thanks. A response of thankfulness is also expressed in joyful words and in happy smiles.

Bible Thoughts for your conversation:

I thank God. Timothy 1:3

Be thankful [to God]. Psalm 100:4

It is . . . good . . . to give thanks to the Lord.
Psalm 92:1

We know that [God] hears us. I John 5:15

STOP! *Before you continue:*

Evaluate your block area by asking yourself—

☐ *Is it located away from where teachers and children must walk?*

☐ *Are the blocks in good condition? Free from splinters and rough edges?*

☐ *Are there enough blocks so several children can build at the same time?*

☐ *In a fours and fives department, are there accessory toys to encourage dramatic play?*

☐ *Are the blocks and accessory toys stored on the open shelves within the child's reach?*

CHAPTER TEN

GOD'S WONDERS, BOOKS AND PUZZLES

Provide a God's Wonders display for Bible Learning Activities (Sunday School) and Choosing Time (Church Time).

Young children are bursting with curiosity! "Let me see!" (touch, taste, hear, smell) is their familiar plea. This act of discovery is an integral part of the young child's world. Exploring God's wonders helps a child begin to sense the extent of God's love, care and wisdom. Through nature experiences he begins to see the patterns and relationships in God's creation.

The wonder and excitement of nature presents a variety of opportunities for you to help the young child learn about God and himself. As he observes the wonder of seeds growing or a butterfly struggling out of its cocoon, he can know that *all things were made by God.*[1] When he sees the beauty in the design of a single snowflake, he can respond naturally by saying, "Thank you, God, for making snowflakes." The child learns to associate God with these experiences as you help him make these relationships. He responds in heart and mind to the greatness of God.

For a child to learn of God's world, he needs to think about it, touch it, taste it, smell it, listen to it and watch it. This firsthand investigation extends his awareness of the natural environment in which he lives; it offers opportunities for you to clarify facts and help him add to what he may already know. At the God's Wonders table, the child learns to share materials, ideas and simple discoveries. He can learn to reason simply and classify ideas and objects. He can begin to learn problem solving. He begins to appreciate beauty.

The God's Wonders display is a place where the child can work and think alone or where he can exchange ideas with a small group of other children. The presence of nature materials often seems to help an insecure child feel more comfortable in a new situation. If there is a live animal at the display, the child often focuses his interest on the animal and forgets himself.

The two year old will approach the God's Wonders display in a very simple way. At first he may pick up an object, look at it from all angles and maybe try to taste it. Then he may put the object down and move on to another activity. Expect him to return to the table several times during the morning and repeat the procedure. As the two year old's knowledge and experiences grow, he will become more familiar with materials and respond more readily to the teacher's questions and suggestions. He will hold the shell to his ear to hear the sound inside. He will want a turn to give a pinch of food to the fish. (Be sure the fish food is then put out of reach. A little child may decide that the fish are still hungry and quickly attempt to remedy the situation!) He will smell the flower or blow the downy feather.

The three year old knows a little about many things. He probably knows that animals can't talk; pinecones come from a tree and plants grow from seeds. He continues to explore the wonders of God's world with increased interest. He is curious about living and growing things. He asks questions. He continues using his senses as a means of discovery.

The four year old wants and needs to do things for himself. This independence gives him an opportunity to test and experiment in his expanding world. He is ready to participate in a few simple experiments such as placing small objects (rock, wood, cork, etc.) in water to determine which ones float or sink to the bottom. The four year old's interest in living things continues, but he begins to show an interest in inanimate objects, such as rocks and magnets.

5 The five year old is ready to experiment. His interests and knowledge of his world have expanded. He is curious. Now he is able to plan and to work in small groups as well as alone. The five year old is still interested in the color and fragrance of a flower, but now he wants to know about the flower's parts. He knows rain falls from the sky and the sun dries it up, but he wants to know where the rain comes from and where it goes. He wants to know how simple machines work, what magnets pick up and what makes a rainbow. The wise teacher will answer the five year old's questions with "Let's find out," rather than supplying the answer. With some guidance from the teacher, he can make many discoveries for himself.

For twos, threes, and younger fours, God's Wonders activities should be completed in a single session. Most fours and fives can participate in activities lasting for longer periods of time. These activities might include growing plants from seeds or watching a caterpillar change into a butterfly.

MATERIALS[2] AND PROCEDURES

Note: Have simple books about rocks, shells, animals, birds, reptiles, etc., clearly and accurately illustrated for a readily available source of information as you guide children in discovering God's Wonders.

Nature walks The children should wear appropriate wraps. Use a walking rope to keep children together. (A walking rope is a length of rope the children hold onto as they walk. Explain clearly and simply its purpose so children know what they are expected to do.) Bring containers for any specimen you find along the way. To make your walk a valuable learning experience, suggest something specific the children can look for. Discuss safety rules, such as walking on the sidewalk and staying with the group.

As you walk along, talk about the things you see. Avoid hurrying the children. Stop for a closer look at flowers, an insect or a rock. Relate what the children see to the orderliness of God's world, His care for the things He has made. "God planned for many trees to lose their leaves in the fall. In the spring the trees will grow new leaves. . . . God planned for birds to build nests. The nest is the bird's home." In the fall, let the children step on the fallen leaves. "How do the leaves sound? . . . How do they feel under your feet?" In the winter find a spot where children can scatter seeds for the birds. Let them smell new flowers in the spring. Help the children understand that the flowers are there for everyone to enjoy. They should not be picked or destroyed. Watch for rocks, insects or leaves the children can bring back to the classroom. In the hot summer months help the children be aware of shady trees and cool water and to express thankfulness to God for these gifts.

Planting Interesting indoor gardens can be grown from parts of fruit and vegetables. Save the top inch of carrots, beets, turnips or rutabagas; also a few potato eyes and an onion. And don't forget those favorites, the avocado seed and the sweet potato. Seeds that will grow quickly are lettuce, radish, lima bean, lentil, grass, nasturtium, pumpkin and melon.

Use unbreakable, wide bottom containers for planters. You will also need a supply of planter mix or soil and newspapers; watering cans. An important accessory in a planting experience is a magnifying glass.

To "plant" a vegetable garden, stand the carrots, beets, turnips, or rutabaga tops in a shallow dish of water. Use small pebbles to support the plant. Within a few days small white roots will appear and fern-like leaves will begin to grow.

Place the sweet potato, pointed end down, in a jar of water. Use a transparent plastic or glass container so roots will be visible. Leave about one-third of the potato above water. Insert several toothpicks if necessary to keep the potato from sinking. The potato will root and in about ten days vines will begin to grow. Avocado seeds and onions can be planted in a similar way.

Young children enjoy planting and watching the growth progress. Seeds can be planted as a group project to be left in the classroom for all to see or in individual containers for each child to take home. If plants are left in the room, arrange for them to be watered during the week. On Sunday let twos and threes use medicine droppers to water plants to prevent their drowning the plants. Older children can easily manage watering cans.

Some seeds should be planted so the children can see them germinate. Roll a piece of blotting paper and put it inside a glass. The paper should touch the sides of the glass. Then fill the center of the glass with damp sand. Slip several lima beans between the paper and the glass. (See sketch.) Keep the sand moist. The children will have a clear view of the roots and root hairs.

Sprinkle grass seed, lettuce or radish seeds on a damp sponge. Place the sponge in a shallow container and keep it moist. The seeds will germinate quickly and the children will be able to see the roots as well as the leaves. Seeds may also be sprinkled on top of a shallow pan of damp soil and kept moist.

A corncob soaked in water and sprinkled with grass seed makes an interesting planter. Lentils sprinkled on a saucer of water will become a green floating garden.

Magnets Have a horseshoe magnet and two bar magnets available for children to use. Bar magnets are excellent for illustrating how like poles (ends) repel and opposite poles attract.

Suspend one bar magnet from a string by tying the strings around the center of the bar. The child holds the other bar magnet and tries to touch one pole (end) of his magnet to the like pole of the suspended magnet. The repelling force will cause the suspended magnet to move away. Opposite poles will pull toward each other.

Provide a variety of objects, some of which will adhere to the magnet and some that will not. Also have two boxes, one marked "yes" and one marked "no." Place a variety of objects in a shallow box or on the table. The child can experiment to see what the magnet will or will not attract. Objects the magnet attracts are placed in the box marked "yes." "Did the magnet attract the paper clip? . . . God planned for magnets to attract objects made of iron or steel."

For further experiments provide a piece of heavy paper, a glass or jar of water, a small pane of glass (bind the edges of the glass with masking tape to prevent cut fingers), a handkerchief, a dish of sand or dirt and paper clips. Ask "Will the magnet attract through a piece of paper? . . . Let's find out." Lay a piece of paper over a paper clip. Use the magnet to lift the paper clip and paper. Repeat the experiment using the pane of glass. Lay the paper clip on top of the paper or pane of glass. Let a child hold the magnet underneath. As the child moves the magnet the paper clip will move. Let a child pick up a paper clip or other iron object with a magnet wrapped in a handkerchief or use a magnet to retrieve a paper clip from a glass of water.

A magnet passed through dirt or sand will pick up the iron filings. Sprinkle some of the filings in a glass of water. The filings will move about in the water as the magnet is moved along the outside of the glass. Place some filings on a sheet of paper. Move the magnet underneath the paper. The iron filings will follow the movement of the magnet.

Children enjoy playing games involving magnets. For "Find the Nail" provide drinking straws, three or four large finishing nails and toothpicks.

Place a nail in each of three or four straws. Place toothpicks in the remaining straws. Bend the ends of the straws to keep the nails and toothpicks from falling out. Place the straws in a box. The children take turns using the magnet to find the straws containing nails.

For a fishing game, provide fish cut from construction paper, a paper clip for each fish and a fishing pole made from a small magnet suspended from a short length of string tied to a piece of dowel. Place a paper clip on the nose of each paper fish. Put the fish in a box or on the floor. The children take turns fishing with the magnet fishing pole.

Water For water play provide plastic aprons, plastic containers, brushes, bubble soap, paper cups, drinking straws, rotary egg beaters, Ivory soap chips (detergents can be harmful to children), small boats and sponges. Accessory toys that make water play more interesting include plastic eyedroppers, funnels, unbreakable measuring cups, squeeze bottles and clothes sprinklers. A few drops of food coloring in the water adds interest.

Ideally, water play should be an outdoor activity. However, with proper protection of the floor and table tops, water play can be a successful indoor activity as well. A large sheet of plastic will protect floors and carpets; newspaper will protect table tops.

Water play should be a part of Vacation Bible School activities for young children. The warm outdoor temperature and a longer time schedule (than Sunday morning) allow children freedom to enjoy this interesting experience.

An apron, a small container of water and a brush is all the equipment needed for the young child to experiment with water painting. He can paint outside walls, sidewalks, outdoor equipment or large sheets of masonite.

Most all young children enjoy blowing bubbles; it requires the simplest of equipment. Mix water with soap chips in paper cups. Give each child a cup of soapy water and a drinking straw. Demonstrate blowing air into the straw. Keep a sponge handy to wipe up spills. The children will also enjoy mixing the soapy water with a rotary beater. A few drops of food coloring will make colorful bubbles.

Moving his hands through water and slowly pouring water from one container to another seems to have a calming effect on most young children. They enjoy the feel and the fun of water. Provide a large plastic tub or basin of water and the accessory toys mentioned previously. The children will experiment pouring, measuring, squirting and washing. Some will be content to just wiggle their fingers in the cool water. They also enjoy bathing dolls, washing dishes and scrubbing table tops. "How does the water feel, Janet? I'm glad God made the cool water. . . . Does this cup hold as much water as that cup, Eric? Which cup holds the most water? You're using the eyes God gave you to see how much water is in each cup."

Fours and fives enjoy experimenting as well as playing with water. For simple experiments with evaporation, place a rubber band around the outside of a glass. Fill the glass with water to the level of the rubber band. The following Sunday check the level of the water. As the children discuss where the water has gone, use the word *evaporated.* Explain simply that evaporated means the water has gone back into the air. A simple chart will help older fives understand God's plan for rain and evaporation.

Water from lakes, sprinklers, etc., evaporate into the air. Rain returns water to the earth. The water evaporates again.

At the beginning of the hour soak two identical cloths in water. Hang one cloth in the sunshine and the other in the shade. Check the cloths throughout the morning and see which one dries first. "The sun helps water evaporate so our clothes dry more quickly. God made the sun." *God made everything!*

For an experiment involving frozen water, give each child a paper cup containing one or two ice cubes. Talk about how the ice feels (cold, hard, wet, slippery) and of what the ice is made. *"Who made the water? . . . All things were made by God! . . .* What is ice? Ice is water that has been frozen solid. Why do we need ice? . . . What happens when ice is not in a refrigerator?" Place the cups outside in the sunshine. At the end of the hour check to see what has happened to the ice.

Children enjoy experimenting with all kinds of objects to determine which objects float and which ones sink. Let the children take turns placing objects (some that float, some that sink—rock, cork, marble, sponge, twig, spoon, etc.) in a large container of water such as an aquarium. As each child puts his object in the water ask, "Does the (feather) sink or float?" Objects sink when they are heavy enough to push aside the water in which they are placed. It is sufficient at this time to simply state, "God made some objects to float and some objects to sink." Give brief, meaningful facts rather than long, dull explanations.

Place two plastic containers with tight fitting covers into the water. "Did the containers float or sink? . . . What do you think will happen if we put marbles in one container? . . . Let's find out." Place a few marbles in one container. Replace the lid and return the container to the water. Add marbles until the container sinks to the bottom. Each time the container is returned to the water ask the children to tell what is happening.

Senses For activities involving the sense of touch, provide a "touch-n-feel" box or bag (cut a hole in the box just large enough for a child's hand); also objects of different sizes, shapes and textures. Select objects the child can easily identify by touch such as a pencil, blunt scissors, ball, comb, spoon and button. Display the touch-n-feel box or bag (with the desired objects inside) at the God's Wonders table. The child reaches through the opening to feel an object. He tries to identify the object without seeing it. Vary this activity by putting a few objects in a cloth bag. The child feels an object through the bag to identify it. "How does the object you are touching feel? . . . Is it hard or soft? . . . Do you know what it is? . . . We use our hands to feel things. God made our wonderful hands."

For another tactile activity gather scraps of material, cut into uniformly shaped pieces (circles or squares, etc.) and put them in a box. Include duplicate pieces. Or mount the pieces in a scrapbook. Select material in a variety of textures such as corduroy, burlap, velvet, flannel, sandpaper, fur, leather, satin, plastic, wire screen, rubber and corrugated paper.

A child can use the cut pieces of materials in several ways. He removes them from the box, examines them and puts them away. He matches duplicate pieces. Most fives are able to classify the pieces according to texture. Two year olds will especially enjoy the texture scrapbook as they turn the pages and feel the material.

For activities involving sight, provide a kaleidoscope, a prism, liquid tempera paint in primary colors, three to five familiar objects, such as a pencil, ball, block or ribbon. Of the numerous activities to help a child become aware of things he can see, one of the most interesting is looking through a kaleidoscope. Another is experimenting with paint to make new colors. The child can put two of the primary (red, yellow, blue) colors in a container and mix them with a brush or ice cream stick. He can experiment further by adding more of one or the other color. Color can also be mixed by dribbling one primary color on top of the other on a sheet of paper. Watch the new color appear as the two primary colors run together. "What happened when you mixed blue and yellow together? . . . Can you think of something God made that is green? . . . God planned many colors for our world. God made our eyes so we can see the beautiful colors." Play a guessing game. Place three to five objects in a row. Ask one child to close his eyes. Remove one object. Ask the child to open his eyes and tell what is missing. Most three year olds can play the game successfully with two or three objects. Fours and fives can play with three to five objects. Place a prism in the sunlight; look at the colors in the rainbow as the light is refracted. Help children name the colors.

For activities involving hearing, provide objects that make sounds, such as a bell, a drum, a baby rattle, a whistle. For older children include scissors and a ball. Ask the children to close their eyes. Make a familiar sound (ring a bell, clap your hands, cut with scissor, etc.) and let the children identify it.

Another activity involving sound will need materials such as sand, beans, rice, marbles, paper clips, etc., and small containers with lids (35 mm film cans are ideal). If possible, provide a tuning fork. Place sand, paper clips, rice, etc., in small containers. Be sure the lids are on tight. As children shake the containers and listen to the sounds, guide their thinking with questions, such as "How does it sound? . . . Is it a loud sound or a soft sound? . . . Which sound is softer? . . . How do we hear sounds? . . . God made our ears."

For activities involving the sense of smell, provide small plastic pill bottles with snap-on lids, cotton and materials with various aromas. These aromas can include peppermint, clove, vanilla and lemon extract, perfume, vinegar, etc. Do not include ammonia, gasoline or pepper. These can be injurious to the child.

Fill small bottles with cotton; saturate cotton with substances that have different aromas. Older children can remove the lids to smell the contents. For twos and threes, punch several very small holes in the lids so they can smell the contents without removing the cap. "God made your nose to smell so many things!"

For activities involving taste provide bite-sized pieces of crackers, fruit and vegetables. Also provide ingredients and equipment to make instant pudding. Let the children sample crackers and bite-sized pieces of fruit and vegetables. "How does it taste? . . . God gave us a tongue so we can taste food." Help children notice the different kinds of food coverings (banana, apple peel, orange rind, etc.).

For children to assist in making instant vanilla pudding, cover table top with newspapers. Mix pudding according to directions. Let children take turns using rotary beater. When pudding is done, spoon small amounts in paper muffin cups for children to eat with plastic spoons.

A Vegetable Man gives children another interesting food experience. Have a pumpkin, newspaper, paring knife, carrot, parsley, two turnips, red bell pepper, toothpicks for attaching vegetable pieces to pumpkin; small pieces of each vegetable for tasting. Gather children around table or on floor to observe pumpkin. Protect work area with newspapers. Encourage use of senses by asking, "What color is our pumpkin? How does it feel? Can you smell it? Does it make a noise?

TURNIP CURL EARS

PARSLEY

TURNIP EYES

CARROT NOSE

RED PEPPER MOUTH

Who made the pumpkin grow? What do you think is inside? Let's cut it open and find out." Cut pumpkin open; also cut a hole for carrot nose. Keep children a safe distance from knife. Let children pull out the seeds. Show threads that hold the seeds to the pumpkin. Ask, "How do the seeds feel?" (Cold, slippery, slimy.) Lay seeds on paper towels to dry. Save dried seeds to plant later.

One at a time, show vegetables. Encourage children to name each one. Offer samples for tasting. With toothpick attach pieces of pared vegetables to pumpkin as shown. Let children arrange parsley "hair." Talk of God's goodness to help us have our food to eat. As the children enjoy this activity, the joy and delight they express is a part of their thanksgiving and praise. A prayer of thanks to God may be another natural response to this experience.

Animal life   There is a wide variety of animal life that can be brought into the classroom. Animal "friends" can range from pill bugs and tadpoles to a child's new puppy. The amount of care and equipment each needs varies. Caterpillars require a cage, a twig on which to crawl and leaves from the tree on which they were found. Insects need similar equipment. Food needs vary. Ladybugs eat aphids. A praying mantis eats aphids, small live insects and raw hamburger. Crickets will eat bread crumbs, a few raisins and even a small amount of lettuce. Grasshoppers will eat almost anything; leaves, orange peel, and toast. All insects need water as well as food.

Frogs, toads, lizards and turtles need a cage with dirt or sand on the bottom. Provide a shallow pan of water. They eat live insects and meal worms.

Fish are easy to care for in a bowl or aquarium. Provide commercially packaged fish food. Birds such as parakeets or canaries are also excellent visitors to Sunday school departments.

Place the insect, animal or bird in an area where the children can view it easily. As the children watch, call their attention to specific things about the insect or animal. "See how the toad flicks out his tongue to catch his food. God made the toad's tongue in a very special way. . . . The caterpillar is beginning to spin his cocoon. He is spinning the thread round and round his body just as God planned." Children can share in the care of animal life by helping clean cages, bringing food and feeding the animal with the teacher's guidance. After a few Sundays of observation, the insects and animals should be returned to their natural habitats.

If a child brings a kitten or puppy to Sunday school, care should be taken to avoid excessive handling. It might be best to arrange for the animal to be taken from the room after Bible Learning Activity Time. This would allow the animal to rest and the children to concentrate on other activities. Guide the children's handling of the animal. Curious little fingers can poke eyes or squeeze too tightly. "Pet the puppy gently. We want to be kind to our puppy friend. . . . How does his fur feel? . . . God made the puppy to have a soft, warm coat."

BIBLE TEACHING/LEARNING OPPORTUNITIES

The child's natural interest and curiosity in God's Wonders provides endless opportunities for the teacher to help him know what God's Word says and how it relates to his life. When your Bible teaching/learning aim involves SHARING, use these ideas and thoughts in your conversation:

"Thank you for sharing your watering can with Ellen, Patty. Now Ellen can give her plant a drink, too. . . I saw Mike sharing the magnifying glass with Kurt at the God's Wonders table. Mike knows our Bible tells us to *share what we have with others*. . . . That's a good idea, Scott. I'm glad you shared it with us."

Bible Thoughts for your conversation:
Share what you have with others. Hebrews 13:16
(The Twentieth Century New Testament)
A friend loves at all times. Proverbs 17:17
Do that which is right and good. Deuteronomy 6:18

KINDNESS

Recognize a child who performs acts of kindness. This means of positive attention reinforces his acceptable behavior. "Sue, you are kind to let Cathy have a turn with the magnet. Our Bible tells us to *be kind to one another. . . .* Steven, you are kind to help Sally wipe the table. When we play with water sometimes spills. . . . You are kind to pet the kitten so gently, Eddie. We want to *be kind* to animals."

Sometimes you'll need to create opportunities for child to show kindness. "Mary, Karen needs to stand closer so she can see our butterfly. What can you do to help her? . . . You are a kind friend to move over so Karen has room. Our Bible tells us to *be . . . kind.*"

Bible Thoughts for your conversation:
Be . . . kind to one another. Ephesians 4:32
Treat everyone with kindness. 2 Corinthians 1:24
Do that which is right and good. Deuteronomy 6:18

HELPING

The young child enjoys helping so long as the tasks are within his ability and interest span. Be alert to ways for him to help at the God's Wonders table. Give one simple suggestion at a time. Commend the child for his work. "Craig may help by giving everyone a cup. Thank you for helping, Craig. . . . You are a kind helper, Amy. Thank you for bringing leaves for the caterpillar. . . . We have fine helpers at our table today. Carl may help by putting the scrapbook on the shelf. Sharon and Tony may put the touch-n-feel book on the shelf. Our Bible says *we are helpers.* When we all help we clean up very quickly."

Bible Thoughts for your conversation:
We . . . are helpers. 2 Corinthians 1:24
I . . . will help. 2 Samuel 10:11

[*With*] *love* [*help*] *one another.* Galatians 5:13
Help each other. Proverbs 12:12 *(The Living Bible)*

CREATION

Plants, elements of weather, and animals are quite naturally related to creation. Other activities at the God's Wonders table can be related to creation, also. It is God who made the hands to feel, the ears to hear, etc. Magnetism, and refraction of light in a prism and the ability of water to support weight are all part of God's handiwork.

"What are you using to smell the lemon, Jack? God made our noses so we can smell lemons and flowers and all kinds of things. *All things were made by God.* . . . What do the plants need to grow? God made the sun and rain to help the plants grow."

Bible Thoughts for your conversation:

[*God*] . . . *made everything beautiful.* Ecclesiastes 3:11

God is good. Psalm 73:1

All things were made by [*God*]. John 1:3

It is [*God*] *who has made us.* Psalm 100:3

The Lord has done great things for us . . . we are glad. Psalm 126:3

God . . . gives rain upon the earth. Job 5:8, 10 *(Berkeley)*

THANKFULNESS

Young children respond naturally to the wonder and awe of God's creation. This response of mind and heart easily becomes one of thankfulness. "How does the rain help us? *God gives rain on the earth.* We can tell God thank you for the rain. . . . *I thank God* for our eyes. Why do we need eyes? . . . This cool water feels good on a hot day like today. We can tell God thank you for the water. Our Bible tells us *it is good to give thanks to the Lord.*"

Bible Thoughts for your conversation:

I thank God. 2 Timothy 1:3

Be thankful to God. Psalm 100:4

O Give thanks to the Lord; for He is good. Psalm 136:1

We know that [*God*] *hears us.* I John 5:15

STOP! *Before you continue:*

Plan a Bible learning activity for the God's Wonders table built on this Bible teaching/learning aim: Teach to help child KNOW God made all things in our world. RESPOND by recognizing and naming things God made for us to eat; by thanking God. Keep in mind the characteristics and abilities of the age child with whom you work. Jot down conversation ideas and Bible Thoughts you might use with the children.

Provide a quiet area where children can look at Books and work Puzzles during Bible Learning Activities (Sunday School) and Choosing Time (Church Time). Books may also be used occasionally during Together Time.

Books are important learning tools for all children. They bring pleasure, create ideas, stimulate curiosity and help children solve problems. Books help the young child develop an awareness of words; he learns that books convey thoughts and ideas. Happy experiences with colorful, interesting books help create a desire to read.

Children enjoy looking at books alone or hearing the book read by the teacher. Books can be used to present a new idea, to reinforce learning or just for fun.

Twos and threes are primarily interested in the pictures. The child will often point to one object in a picture and name it. Although younger children are usually anxious to go on to the next page, they enjoy responding to your simple questions about the picture. Twos probably will answer with one word, while threes respond in a phrase or a simple sentence. Teachers can help build vocabulary by repeating the child's reply in a complete sentence and sometimes adding a descriptive word. "What is this, Karen? . . . That's right. It's a cat. It's a yellow cat. God made the yellow cat." Since twos and threes are yet quite self-centered, they like to hear stories about familiar objects and experiences.

Fours and fives look primarily at the pictures in a book, but also enjoy hearing the story. They are increasingly aware of the words on the page. A child may ask, "What does this word say?" Five year olds are learning to recognize some words and may happily announce, "I know that word! That word is 'stop'." Fours and fives increased attention span allows them to enjoy longer stories than when they were younger.

Encourage fours and fives to use books for research. "There is a book about insects on our book shelf. Let's see if it tells about this ladybug."

MATERIALS[1]

Books   Select picture books with large, clear, colorful pictures and a minimum of detail. Books for twos and threes should have a few words on each page. Stories should be about familiar subjects, such as animals, babies and families; and about familiar activities, such as playing, helping, eating and sleeping. Books for fours and fives should also include pictures and stories about nature, machines and children from other lands. Simple stories about Jesus can be included for all ages.

Bindings on all books must be sturdy. Books should be kept on a bookshelf accessible to the children.

PROCEDURE

Limit the number of books you display. Too many simply confuse a child. Change the books at the beginning of each unit of lessons. Select books from those listed in your *Leader's/Teacher's Manual.*

Books should be attractively arranged in a quiet area of the room where a child can browse through a book alone or join two or three others to listen to a story. Unless a teacher is nearby to read the text or talk about the picture, a child has "seen" a book in a few seconds.

As you look at a picture book with a child, ask questions that will stimulate observation and thought. "What sound does a dog make? . . . What is the kitten wearing around its neck? . . . Why do you think the girl looks sad?"

To encourage responsibility in caring for books, show the child how to turn pages carefully; also to return the book to the shelf when he has finished.

Place an appropriate book at an interest center and encourage the children to use it for reference. "This book is about many different kinds of rocks. Maybe we can find a picture of our rocks in the book."

When reading to fours and fives explain the meaning of the word *title* and use the word when you begin the story. "The title of this story is . . ." Explain the job of the author and the illustrator.

Keep a Picture Bible[1] in the book area. Young children can know that the Bible is a special book that tells us about God and the Lord Jesus. They will enjoy looking through the Bible and recognizing pictures that illustrate a favorite story. Bible story books with clear, accurate pictures help children know of Bible-time customs, clothing, homes, etc.

PUZZLES

"Look! I did it!" Scott shouts as he completes a wooden inlay puzzle. Puzzles help satisfy a child's desire to achieve. They provide an opportunity for the child to work alone or with one or two friends. When a child uses puzzles he learns to think, to reason and to solve problems. He learns to work independently. Working puzzles helps develop eye-hand coordination. Through using puzzles a child can enjoy a sense of achievement. He learns to share and take turns.

The attention span and coordination of most twos allows them to use puzzles with only three or four pieces. Each puzzle piece is a picture of a whole object (a bunny, a ball, etc.). He will press the piece against the puzzle frame, maneuvering it until it falls into place. Threes, fours and fives can work puzzles with more pieces, not necessarily representing a whole object. The complexity of the puzzle used depends upon the child's coordination and dexterity, not necessarily his age.

MATERIALS

Wooden inlay puzzles are excellent for young children. Puzzles for twos should have only three or four pieces. As children become experienced they will be able to work increasingly difficult puzzles. Most fours and fives can work puzzles with ten or more pieces.

Puzzles can be purchased or made. They should be colorful with a simple picture and large pieces. They should be stored in a puzzle rack or on a low shelf.

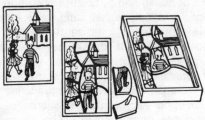

PROCEDURE

There will probably be children in each age group who need simple puzzles with only three or four pieces. As the child works these puzzles over and over again he will gain confidence and be able to proceed to more complicated ones. Have a more difficult puzzle ready and waiting for that moment. "Allen, you completed that puzzle so quickly and so easily! I have a new puzzle for you. It's a little bit harder, but I know you can do it." Remain nearby to give encouragement. Praise the child's accomplishments.

If a child is becoming frustrated in his attempts to complete a puzzle, step in with suggestions that will allow him the satisfaction of completing the puzzle on his own. "I wonder if the piece will fit if you turn it around? . . . This part of the puzzle is red. Can you find a red piece that will fit right here?"

Give the child the responsibility of returning the puzzle to its proper place when he is finished.

BIBLE TEACHING/LEARNING OPPORTUNITIES

When your lesson's Bible teaching/learning aim involves "Sharing," "Kindness" or "Helping," select books with stories about children who demonstrate these kinds of behavior. In your conversation encourage the child to talk about what is happening in the story or pictures and relate the happenings to Scripture truth. "What is the boy doing? . . . When we rake the leaves we are helping. Our Bible tells us to *help each other*."

Use puzzles that have pictures of children helping. "The girl in your puzzle is using her hands to help. What is she doing? God made our hands to help."

The use of books and puzzles provide opportunities for children to share, to help and to be kind. "Mary, you are kind to move over so Kenny can see the book, too. . . . Marilyn, thank you for sharing your puzzle with Paula. Our Bible tells us to *share what you have with others*. . . . Bobby, you are putting the books on the shelf very neatly. You are a fine helper."

Bible Thoughts for your conversation:

Help each other. Proverbs 12:12 *(The Living Bible)*

Children, obey your parents . . . for this is right.
Ephesians 6:1

Share what you have with others. Hebrews 13:16
(The Twentieth Century New Testament)

Treat everyone with kindness. Galatians 6:10

Be kind toward one another. Ephesians 4:32
(Berkeley)

CREATION

When you use picture books about animals and nature for twos and threes, ask "What do you see in this picture? Who made the puppy? . . . What is growing on the tree? (To give young children a clue, point to the object in the picture as you mention it.) God planned for apples to grow on trees."

As fours and fives use books to learn more about objects on the God's Wonders table, use these thoughts and ideas in your conversation. "Bees carry pollen from flower to flower. God planned for bees to help new plants to grow. . . . The tiny sea animal that lived in this shell built his shell larger and larger as he grew. God planned it that way."

In the Picture Bible point out Bible words that are related to creation. "This is the part of the Bible that tells us that God made our beautiful world. Right here it says *'God made the sky.'* . . . See the words marked with red? They tell us that *all things were made by God."*

Bible Thoughts for your conversation:

God . . . made the world and everything in it.
   Acts 17:24

God . . . gives us . . . all things to enjoy.
   I Timothy 6:17

There is nothing too hard for [God]. Jeremiah 32:17

All things were made by [God]. John 1:3

THANKFULNESS

Include in your book selections of stories about prayer. In your conversation use these thoughts and ideas. "What is the little girl holding? . . . We can tell God thank you for the flowers. . . . Why did the boy in our story tell God thank you? . . . Yes, he was glad that God helped his friend get well. . . . We can tell God thank you for books to read. We can tell Him thank you for making our eyes so we can read books."

Bible Thoughts for your conversation:

I thank God. 2 Timothy 1:3

O Give thanks to the Lord; for He is good. Psalm 136:1

It is good . . . to give thanks to the Lord. Psalm 92:1

Be thankful [to God]. Psalm 100:4

STOP! Before you continue, ask yourself these questions:

☐ *Is my bookshelf and puzzle table in a quiet area of the room?*

☐ *Do the contents of the books on my bookshelf relate to the current unit's Bible teaching/-learning aim?*

☐ *Are my puzzles in good condition with no pieces missing?*

CHAPTER ELEVEN

HOME LIVING

Provide Home Living activities for Bible Learning Activities (Sunday School) and Choosing Time (Church Time).

A child readily identifies himself with the person, situation or environment with which he has had satisfying firsthand experience. For the young child, this means his family and life in his own home. Therefore your home living area provides natural opportunities for a child to play out familiar, everyday experiences.

Home living activities also provide opportunities for the child to work off energy and release tensions in acceptable ways. Rocking, lifting, setting the table, etc. use both large and small muscles and help develop muscles coordination. The child can play out feelings and anxieties, try out adult roles, clarify concepts and the meanings of words. Children often act out an illness, a trip to the doctor or having "shots." A child with a new baby at home may hit a doll or throw it on the floor—something he would like to do, but knows he must not do to his new brother or sister. He may play out a frightening experience, such as being separated from his parents.

The boy who dresses in a man's hat and coat, eats breakfast and leaves for work is experimenting with how it feels to be a daddy. Girls take on the role of mother as they care for babies and work with home living equipment.

The home living area is an appropriate place for the young child to practice Christian concepts, such as sharing, helping, taking turns and being kind. He can express thankfulness to God as he prays before eating his "pretend" meal or putting the baby to bed.

By listening as well as observing at the home living area, the alert teacher can gain new insight into what a child is feeling and how he is interpreting the situations he encounters. The child's actions reveal clues as to his interests, his abilities, how he sees himself, what things are bothering him and his understanding of concepts being taught.

The two year old's play is simple. He may be content to simply rock the baby, feed the baby or put the baby to bed. He may want to be the baby; sitting in the toy high chair or lying in the doll bed. He plays alone, involving no one else in his activity. Since his command of words is limited, he often uses his play as a means of expressing ideas.

During his years of three, four and five, his experiences increase, he becomes more verbal and his play becomes more complex. He spends additional time at his play and needs extra "props" such as dress-up clothes and accessories. As he learns to interact with other children, those in the home living area become a "family." Daddy goes to work. Mother cares for the family. Friends come to visit. The child is able to express more of his ideas with words.

MATERIALS

Equipment for the home living area should be child-size rather than doll-size. Include a stove, refrigerator, bed, table, chairs, sink, rocking chair. Home corner furniture can be purchased from educational equipment firms or made from crates and boxes.[1] Furnishings should include unbreakable dishes, empty food containers (cans—carefully washed and dried—boxes, etc.), pots and pans, a child-size broom and a telephone. Dress-up clothes are an important part of home living play. Include dresses, hats, scarves, jewelry, shoes and purses.

It is important that accessory toys also include items with which boys can play out their masculine role. Too often rooms for young children are geared to the tastes and interests of girls rather than boys.

To help boys identify with male roles, provide materials that will encourage masculine kinds of play. Include men's jackets, hats, neckties, a briefcase, discarded camera, binoculars, toolboxes, lunch boxes, billfolds and keys. (Of course, one of the best ways to offer boys the opportunity for male identification is to recruit men teachers!)

PROCEDURE

The teacher arranges the materials in the home living area before the children arrive. He then becomes an interested observer, stepping into the activity to:

- Relate the lesson's Bible teaching/learning aim to the child's interest and activity.
- Help a shy child enter the activity.
- Settle a dispute or aid the children in solving a problem.
- Insure the safety and well-being of the children.

Since dramatic play is free and spontaneous, the children will become involved as their needs and interests dictate. Encourage a shy child to participate by suggesting the use of a specific piece of equipment; also a role the child can assume. "Karen, this family needs a sister to rock the baby to sleep. You can sit in the rocker and rock the baby."

A special accessory and a suggestion from the teacher can guide the child's play toward a specific aim without interfering with the spontaneous dramatic play. For instance, a "letter" delivered to the home corner might tell the children visitors are coming and encourage play involving kindness to visitors. When the lesson aim involves thankfulness for food, a small basket, some crackers and apple slices might help the children play out having a picnic. As you plan for home living activities ask yourself, "Will this activity help accomplish the lesson's Bible teaching/planning aims?"

A few minutes before concluding Bible Learning Activity Time, warn children in the home living area, "It's almost clean-up time." Use positive statements to encourage clean up. "Jack, the dishes belong on this shelf. . . . You are folding the clothes very neatly, Jane. . . . Let's stack the food cans on this shelf. I'll help you."

BIBLE TEACHING/LEARNING OPPORTUNITIES

A teacher can use the young child's natural interest in home living activities to build basic Christian concepts. When your lesson's Bible teaching/learning aim involves "Sharing," use these ideas and thoughts in your conversation:

"Karen is sharing dinner with her visitors. Our Bible tells us to *share what you have with others*. . . . Peter, I'm glad you shared the doll with Kim. Sharing is a way to show love." As a child actually shares materials and ideas, he can more fully understand the meaning of the word, share.

Bible Thoughts for your conversation:
Love one another. I John 4:7

Share what you have with others. Hebrews 13:16
(The Twentieth Century New Testament)
A friend loves at all times. Proverbs 17:17

KINDNESS
Thoughtfulness and kindness become meaningful to a child as he puts these concepts into action or sees others exhibiting kind deeds. Of course, a teacher must be nearby to identify these acceptable ways of behavior, to commend and encourage children in their attitudes and actions; to share their enthusiasm and interests. "Sue, you are a kind mother. You are taking good care of your family. . . . Dan is a kind helper. Our Bible tells us to *be kind to one another*."

Bible Thoughts for your conversation:
Be . . . kind to one another. Ephesians 4:32

Treat everyone with kindness. Galatians 6:10

Do that which is right and good. Deuteronomy 6:18

A man that has friends must show himself friendly.
Proverbs 18:24

HELPING

The home living area provides many opportunities for helping. The "children" help "Mother" set the table. Sister helps iron clothes. "Everyone is helping in our home today. We have happy homes when everyone helps. Our Bible reminds us that *we . . . are helpers.*"

At Helping Time the children who are working at the home living area help put away equipment. "Marcia knows just where to put the dishes. You are a fine helper. . . . David, you may help by putting blankets on the bed. Our Bible says *I will help.*"

Bible Thoughts for your conversation:
We . . . are helpers. 2 Corinthians 1:24

I . . . will help. 2 Samual 10:11

Be willing and obedient. Isaiah 1:19

[With] love, [help] one another. Galatians 5:13

CREATION

The young child can understand that God made him and that living together in families is part of God's plan. Include in your reference to families those composed of one parent, a grandmother, aunt or whoever cares for the child. Make sure no child feels his family situation is unacceptable to you. (Do you know who are the family members of each child in your class? Department?)

"Beth, you are a good mother to your baby. God planned for us to have (mothers and daddies) to take care of us. . . . Bill is using his strong arms to sweep the floor. God made our arms. *It is God who has made us.*"

Bible Thoughts for your conversation:

God . . . made everything. Ecclesiastes 3:11

The Lord is good to all. Psalm 145:9

All . . . things were made by [God]. John 1:3

It is [God] who has made us. Psalm 100:3

God . . . gives us . . . all things to enjoy. I Timothy 6:17

THANKFULNESS

As children play out familiar activities they can be guided to respond quite naturally in thanks to God for food, family, home, church, friends, etc. "What do we do before we eat our dinner? Steve, you are the daddy in our family. You may tell God thank you for the good food. . . . I saw a happy family in our 'home' today. God planned for us to have happy times with our families. We can tell God thank you for our families. Our Bible tells us to *be thankful to God.*"

Bible Thoughts for your conversation:

I thank God. 2 Timothy 1:3

Be thankful [to God]. Psalm 100:4

We know that [God] hears us. I John 5:15

It is . . . good . . . to give thanks to the Lord.
Psalm 92:1

STOP! *Before you continue:*
Evaluate your home living area by asking yourself:

- ☐ *Are there enough dolls, utensils and other materials so several children can play at the same time?*
- ☐ *Are there materials and dress-up clothes that will encourage boys to assume masculine roles?*
- ☐ *Are there sufficient storage areas so children can easily put away materials and equipment in an orderly manner?*

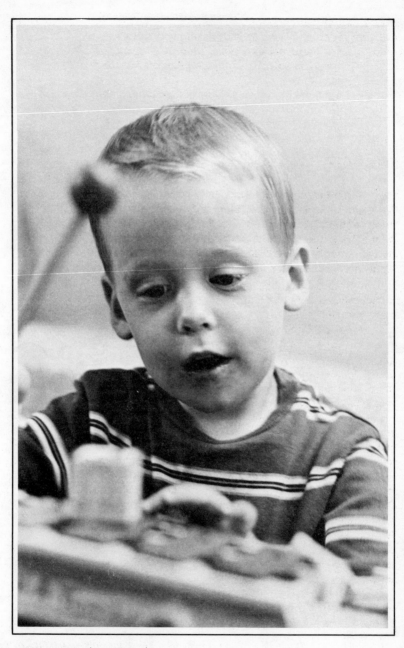

CHAPTER TWELVE

STORYTELLING AND MUSIC

Storytelling takes place during Bible Learning Activity Time and Bible Story Time (Sunday School); also during Together Time and Tell-Me-Time (Church Time). In the Two Year Old departments storytelling takes place throughout the morning whenever a child or small group of children indicate an interest.

Storytelling, a teaching method centuries old, has many values for the young child. It helps the child learn to listen and thus increases his attention span. Listening to stories helps develop the child's ability to retain a sequence of ideas. It gives him experience in speaking and helps increase his vocabulary as he talks about stories he has heard. Storytelling helps a child know of times, places and people that are outside his own experience.

One purpose of storytelling in the Sunday school is to share the gospel of God's love and the effect of this love on lives of all mankind. The Bible is the source of our stories. We want the young child to learn to love God's Word. Therefore, we tell him stories that are within his interest and that reflect a bit of his own everyday experiences. The world of a young child involves experiences with his home, family, a few animals, nature, church, and modes of travel. Bible stories must be based on some part of this experience in order to begin with something he knows.

Stories need to be told in words that mean exactly what they say. Stories that emphasize fear and cruelty threaten a child's feeling of security.

In addition to stories from the Bible, present-day stories are an effective teaching tool for communicating Scripture truths to young children. For instance, each Tell-Me-Time story in your *Leader's/Teacher's Manual* is based on that lesson's Bible teaching/learning aim. Each story illustrates, within a child's interest and experience, a specific Bible truth. The "Let's Talk About the Story" section following each story includes conversation ideas, a Bible Thought, song, prayer—all to help reinforce the Bible truth upon the child's mind and heart.

The attention span of many two year olds does not enable them to sit with a group to listen to a story. Therefore, tell the Bible story many times throughout the morning whenever and wherever one or more children show an interest. Even when twos can participate in group experiences this practice should continue. Twos need—and like—to hear the story again and again.

A three year old's attention span allows him to listen to longer stories. Most threes can listen as part of a group. They, too, need to see pictures and objects to clarify the story's words.

Four and fives are ready for stories of strange places and things if some part of the story contains reference to familiar people, happenings or objects. They are interested in the action of a story—the "what" and the "how." The names of people and places, the dates of events (the "where," "who" and "when") have little meaning to young children.

MATERIALS

The most important piece of equipment needed for Bible storytelling is your Bible! Hold your Bible or keep it open nearby so the children recognize it as the source of your story. Your *Leader's/Teacher's Manual* is also important, but use it for study during the week, not on Sunday morning. Visual resources such as pictures, Bible story figures and puppets can be used to visualize a story. These resources reinforce and give meaning to your words. For a child who has never seen a sheep or a well, pictures are essential to his learning.

PROCEDURE

Begin your story preparation early in the week. Read the story from the Bible. Read it again from one of the modern translations. Avoid the temptation to skip reading the story in the Bible "because I know it so well."

Next, read the story in your *Leader's/Teacher's Manual*. This will help you tell the story in words the child will understand. It is also a guide for the use of specific visual resources.

Several times during the week practice telling the story and using the visual resources. If you feel it is necessary to use notes, write them on a small card and place them in your Bible. But know the story well enough so you can look directly at the children most of the time, with only an occasional glance at your notes.

When telling the story see that the children are seated comfortably and can easily see any visuals you are using. Be sure distractions, such as toys, books or purses are out of sight. To help children get ready to listen, catch their attention with a finger fun[1] or simple action song. Pause briefly as you look into each child's eyes, then begin with the opening sentence of your story.

Tell the story in your normal voice. Speak with confidence and enjoyment; let your genuine interest in the story come through. Also speak clearly, distinctly and slowly. Change the tone of your voice to identify different characters in the story. Create excitement by speaking slightly faster. Whisper or pause briefly to create suspense. "The shepherds hurried down the streets of Bethlehem. Faster and faster they walked. When they came to the stable they went inside. They saw Mary and Joseph. And in the manger they saw (pause) the baby Jesus!"

To keep children's interest use repetition and action verbs. "Step-step-step went Joseph's feet along the dusty road. Steppity, steppity, step. Little Jesus hurried to catch up. . . . Peter's friends helped him pull in the heavy nets of fish. Pull . . . pull . . . pull.

They used their strong arms to pull the nets." Tell your story with expression. Look angry or frightened. Yawn. Smile a big smile.

When the story ends, use your closing sentence and stop! Keep your listening period within the child's attention span.

BIBLE TEACHING/LEARNING OPPORTUNITIES

Your Bible story should be chosen to fit the Bible teaching/learning aim of your lesson. For example, if your Bible teaching/learning aim involves SHARING, KINDNESS or HELPING, your story might be "Feeding the Five Thousand,"[2] "The Woman at the Well"[3] or "Jesus Stilling the Storm."[4] If your aim involves CREATION, your story could be a portion from Genesis. If your aim involves THANKFULNESS, your story might be one that illustrates God's loving care, such as Jacob's dream.[5] The Bible stories in your *Leader's/ Teacher's Manual* have been carefully selected to illustrate the lesson aim. The wise teacher will use these stories consistently and in the way the manual suggests.

STOP! Before you continue, evaluate your last Sunday's storytelling by asking yourself the questions:

- [ ] *Did the story hold the children's attention?*
- [ ] *Did I know the story well enough to have lots of eye contact with the children?*
- [ ] *Did I stop when the story ended?*
- [ ] *Was I well enough prepared in the use of my visual resources so they did not distract from the story?*
- [ ] *Was my story within the understanding and interest of the children?*
   Keep the results of your evaluation in mind as you prepare your story for next Sunday.

Use Singing throughout the entire Sunday School and Church Time program. Use listening activities most often during Bible Learnng Activities (Sunday School) and Choosing Time (Church Time).

Few sounds in a church are as delightful as that of young children singing. Music is a natural expression of their feelings and experiences. When a child feels secure and relaxed, he will often sing or hum spontaneously as he plays. Through music a shy child can become involved in group activity; an over-stimulated, tense child can be helped to relax; an overactive, aggressive child can release his tensions in an acceptable way.

Young children are naturally creative. Observe a group of children involved in play and you will notice that they make up their own songs, chants and games as they play. They respond to the rhythm of a swing, a jump rope or the wind. Music is an outlet for this creativity and a means of self-expression. With the aid of music a child can become a horse or a butterfly, an elephant or a clown. He can use his hands, his feet or his whole body to express how the music makes him feel. **Through music he can work off his energy and stretch large muscles in acceptable ways.**

Music can help children get acquainted and establish friendly feelings. Simple musical games using the child's name can help the child feel accepted. As the children gathered together for group time, Mrs. Martin began to sing "Here we are together. . . . There's Karen and Tommy and Peter and Robin. . . ." [6] Hearing his own name helped each child feel an important part of the group.

Music is a valuable teaching tool to enrich the learning experiences of the child. Meaningful words set to music can create vivid thought pictures and establish scriptural truths that the child's mind and heart will long love and remember. Songs about God, Jesus, creation, thankfulness, helping, sharing and being kind are a means of teaching and reinforcing basic Christian concepts. Music provides the child with opportunities to respond to God in thankfulness and love. As the children looked at a snowflake through a magnifying glass, Mrs. Thomas softly sang, "Thank you, God, I thank you, God. Thank you, God, for snowflakes."[6]

The two year old will usually just watch and listen as you sing. When he has heard a song several times he will begin to respond by singing an occasional word or phrase. When the song includes actions he will often respond with a few of the motions. He enjoys hearing the same songs again and again.

The three year old is beginning to sing with the teacher, though he may be a few words behind. He enjoys singing familiar songs and will often ask "Sing it again." Threes enjoy action songs and simple rhythm activities, even though they cannot yet keep accurate time.

Fours and fives enjoy singing with other children. They like using rhythm instruments. Fours and fives can make their own simple songs about what they've seen or done. Most fives have the ability to sing words and do motions at the same time.

There is no "song service" in a department for young children. Rather, music is used naturally and informally to help children learn specific Bible truths.

MATERIALS

Note: *The songs suggested in your* Leader's/Teacher's Manual *have been carefully selected to help young children learn basic Bible truths. The thoughtful teacher will learn and use these songs consistently as he presents God's Word in a variety of interesting and meangingful ways.*

The basic materials for using music are a source of appropriate songs[6] and your own voice. Songs for the young child should be short, rhythmic and tuneful. The words should be related to the child's interests and experiences. The teacher needs to have many songs on the tip of his tongue. On a moment's notice he might need a helping song, a thank-you song or an activity song.

All departments for young children need a sturdy, easy-to-operate phonograph and a selection of activity records[7] and listening records.

Rhythm instruments are an important musical tool. Rhythm instruments can be purchased or made.[8] They should include drums, wood blocks, bells, rhythm sticks, tambourines and shakers. Five year olds can make some of these rhythm instruments as a Bible learning activity.

An autoharp is an ideal instrument for accompanying young children's singing. Better yet, use no accompaniment at all. Your own voice, your knowledge of appropriate songs, plus your enthusiasm and interest are all the tools you need to use music effectively with young children.

PROCEDURE

At activity centers, teachers should be ready with songs related to the lesson aim. As the children plant seeds, the teacher might sing softly "Who made the seeds? God did. . . ."[6] While children work with collage materials, the teacher might comment that the children are using the hands God made for them, then sing "Thank you, God. I thank you, God. Thank you, God, for my hands."[6]

Music can be used during Bible Story Time to relate a Bible story truth to the child's everyday experience. For example, at the conclusion of the story about Jesus calling His helpers the teacher used the Bible verse *Come, learn of me.* As the children completed invitations asking friends to Sunday school, the teacher sang "Come, learn of Me. Come, learn of Me. Come, learn of Me, Jesus said."[6]

During Together Time, children and teachers sing songs to arouse feelings of reverence, quietness and thoughtfulness. They might sing "We are in our church today . . ." or "We're giving . . . because we love Jesus."[6]

When children become restless or inattentive the wise teacher sings an activity song that allows the children to stretch and move tired muscles. Mrs. Black knew the children needed a change from quiet listening. So she began singing "Let me show you how I clap hands . . ."[6] The children began to sing with her. They sang the song several times using a variety of actions, such as stretching high, hopping and bending low. The concluding verse "Let me show you how I sit tall . . ."—helped the children get ready for the next activity.

To introduce a new song use pictures or objects to illustrate the words. Let the children hear you sing the song several times before you ask them to sing it with you. Suggest that five year olds listen for a certain word or phrase as you sing. Never ask children to "sing as loud as you can."

A song will catch the attention of children more quickly than a spoken command. Announce clean-up with a song, such as "Time to put away your blocks, trucks and dolls and all your toys. . . ."[6] While children put away materials the teacher might sing "I can help pick up my toys. . . ."[6]

Listening records[7] help children relax during Rest Time. Interesting pictures may result when instrumental music is played while children finger-paint or paint at easels.

BIBLE TEACHING/LEARNING OPPORTUNITIES

When your Bible teaching/learning aim involves "Sharing," "Kindness" or "Helping" use these ideas:

Provide activities and games that encourage conduct pleasing to the Lord "because we love Him." Jack and Diane were rolling the ball back and forth. Mrs. Allen said, "I like the way you are sharing the ball. It's fun to play when we share." As the children continued rolling the ball, she sang, "I can share toys with my friends. . . ."[6]

Use songs such as "Showing Love" and "Ways I Help" to emphasize kindness, sharing, taking turns and obeying. These songs are particularly effective because their structure allows you to substitute a word or phrase to include an idea specifically related to a child's experience.

Bible Thoughts for your conversation:

Be . . . kind to one another. Ephesians 4:32
Share what you have with others. Hebrews 13:16
(The Twentieth Century New Testament)
Help each other. Proverbs 12:12

CREATION

As children observe the wonders of God revealed in nature, music can enrich this learning experience. The children went for a walk on a warm spring day. They stopped to look at the blossoming trees and listen to the singing birds. As they looked and listened, the teacher sang "God made our wonderful world . . ."[6]

As twos and threes watched fish in the aquarium, the teacher sang, "Who made the fish? God did. . . ."[6]

Bible Thoughts for your conversation:

God is good. Psalm 73:1

All things were made by [God]. John 1:3

God . . . made the world and everything in it.
Acts 17:24

THANKFULNESS

Music is a natural way for children to express their thankfulness to God. A child may want to express thanks to God several times throughout the morning. Prayers and songs of thanks are not limited to a specific time in the schedule. Children arranging a bouquet of spring flowers might sing, "Thank you, God. I thank you, God. Thank you, God, for pretty flowers."[6]

The children were finger painting. Mr. Anderson said, "I'm glad God planned so many bright colors for our world. It's good to tell God thank you for the pretty colors." As the children worked, Mr. Anderson sang, "It's good to give thanks to the Lord. . . ."[6]

Bible Thoughts for your conversation:

It is . . . good . . . to give thanks to the Lord.
Psalm 92:1

I thank God. 2 Timothy 1:3

We know that [God] hears us. 1 John 5:15

STOP! *Before you continue, do these two things:*

☐ *Note the Bible teaching/learning aim of your current unit of lessons. Learn a song to reinforce this aim. Find suitable pictures to visualize the song.*

☐ *Learn an activity song that will allow the children to stretch and move.*

ART ACTIVITIES

Provide art activities during Bible Learning Activities (Sunday School) and Choosing Time (Church Time).

Art activities offer the young child an opportunity to give expression to what he thinks and feels. A happy, secure child may express his happiness through the bright colors he uses in his easel painting. A shy or inhibited child may express his feelings by making just a few timid strokes with one finger on his finger painting. An angry child may release his emotions by pounding, squeezing or twisting clay.

Through art experiences a child can enjoy feelings of accomplishment. Art is a medium in which he can explore and experiment. He can shape his materials to his own liking. The child builds self-confidence when he proudly says, "Look what I made!" It is his experience, not his completed product that makes his art activity valuable to his growth and development.

Art experiences help heighten the child's awareness of his physical environment. Activities, such as making a collage, allow the child to handle different materials. He becomes involved in exploring colors, textures, shapes and patterns. When he works with dough, he discovers it is pliable—it can be pulled, rolled, pinched and poked. He feels its consistency. He learns that the consistency changes if he works with it a long time, leaves it out of its container or adds water to it. These experiences help the young child begin to understand God's world and his relationship to it.

To help a child become more self-confident and sure of his worth as an individual, he needs a teacher who is friendly and understanding about his art work. A child who is sure of his own value and place in the world finds it easier to accept God's love and to show love to others. As he works at art activities the child can learn basic Christian concepts of sharing, taking turns, being kind and helping others. He has opportunities to learn respect for the ideas and work of those about him.

As a child and teacher use art materials together in a relaxed, creative way, opportunities for natural conversation with the child are likely to come. These "teachable moments" often are the best opportunities to help a child learn basic and vital scriptural truths.

As in other areas of growth, the child progresses through a certain pattern of development in artistic expression. And, as in other areas of growth, he passes through these stages at his own speed.

The first stage in artistic development is called the *manipulative* stage. This stage begins when the child first begins to use crayons, paint or clay. It is a time of exploration; a time of manipulating materials. He discovers what happens when he moves a crayon across a piece of paper or squeezes a piece of clay. He discovers how the materials look, smell, feel and taste.

The child's pictures at this stage are scribbles. As his muscle control improves, he is able to stop and start a line whenever he wants to. Eventually, his scribbling takes on a circular pattern. He is not interested in making anything specific and color is not important to him.

Twos, threes and some fours are usually in this manipulative stage of development. Most young children will return to this stage when introduced to new materials for the first time. A child's work should not be considered "babyish" nor should he ever be told to "Draw something nice. Don't just scribble!"

From the manipulative stage the child progresses to the *controlled* stage. He begins to realize that he has some ability to regulate his materials. He learns that he can use glue to make materials stick together; that clay can be patted into shapes or pinched into pieces. He learns that he can make a line go a certain direction by moving his crayon a certain way.

Next the child enters the *naming* stage. He begins to use words to describe what he makes. At first, the adult may be able to see no resemblance between the object pictured and what the child says it represents. However, his symbols are in constant change, and eventually the resemblance will become apparent. However, recognizing what the child has made is not what matters. The teacher's role is to encourage the child and help him feel pride in his creation. Comments such as, "I like the bright colors in your picture, Greg," or "You certainly worked hard on your painting. You know about painting!" show your acceptance of the child's work.

The child creates what he thinks or feels. He will unconsciously enlarge, distort or change an object or portion of an object depending upon its importance to him. For instance, in a picture of a person picking flowers, the hand may be larger than normal because the hand is important in picking and holding the flowers. A child who feels he is not wanted or not important may often draw himself very small in relation to other family members in his picture.

MATERIALS[1] AND PROCEDURE

When you introduce a new art activity, demonstrate the use of materials. Then remove your work. Some children might tend to copy your efforts and thus miss out on using their own creativity.

Painting   An apron or a smock for each child is a must for all painting activities. A smock can be made easily from a man's shirt. Cut off the sleeves to make them the right length for a child. The child wears the shirt backwards so it buttons down the back. Sponges and soapy water for cleanup are also necessary for all painting activities.

Materials for finger painting includes finger paint and a surface on which to paint. Finger paint may be purchased, but can also be made easily and inexpensively from liquid starch and liquid or dry tempera. The surface on which to paint can be finger paint paper, slick butcher or shelf paper, a formica or enamel table top, a large tray or a piece of oil cloth.

Finger painting is an experience in itself. Fingers, hands and arms smear, squiggle and squish the paint over the paper. The entire creation can be wiped out in a moment if the child desires. Most children enjoy simply moving the paint around on a smooth surface and do not feel the need to make a picture.

Pour about three or four tablespoonsful of liquid starch on the painting surface. Add the amount of paint desired (about one tablespoon). More starch or paint can be added, if necessary, as the child works. Too much starch makes the surface "soupy." The child will mix the starch and paint as he works. Starch and tempera kept in squeeze bottles are ideal for finger painting because the contents can be squirted directly on the work surface without unscrewing lids or spilling paint accidentally. Children should be allowed to work freely without interruption from the teacher. Interesting designs may result when music is played while children paint. Remember that the experience and enjoyment of finger painting is more important than the end results. If a child wants a picture to take home, lay a clean piece of paper over the finger painting, rub the paper lightly and pull it off.

Provide pans of warm, soapy water for cleanup. Let the child soak his hands in the water for a few minutes when his work is finished. His hands will come clean with very little scrubbing and he will enjoy the feel of the warm water.

For easel painting, provide paper, large brushes, liquid tempera, paint containers and easels. Paper should be 18" by 24". Newsprint, manila, butcher paper and the want ad section from the newspaper can all be used. Brushes should have long handles— about ten to twelve inches—and wide, soft bristles. Liquid tempera paint, available from art supply stores or educational material firms, is convenient and easy to use. It can be thinned with water, liquid starch or liquid soap, if necessary. Powdered tempera is less expensive to buy, but it is also less convenient, since it has to be mixed into a liquid. Powdered tempera can be mixed with water or liquid starch or a combination of both. The prepared mixture should be the consistency of heavy cream. A few drops of liquid soap added to the paint makes cleanup easier. Paint containers can include empty frozen juice or soup cans, baby food jars with screw tops or ½ pint milk cartons with the tops removed. The lids on baby food jars keep the paint from drying out overnight. Easels can be purchased in either wood or aluminum, but substitutes can be made from cardboard, pegboard or Masonite.[1] If necessary, the children can paint on tables.

Easel painting is a favorite art activity of the young child. The teacher's part in easel painting is to provide materials and an environment that will allow the child freedom in creativity. Before he begins to paint, print his name on the back of his paper. Twos should begin with only one color. As their experience with easel painting increases the number of paints they use may increase. Fours and fives may use from six to eight colors. The child needs instruction on how to drag his brush along the edge of the container to prevent dripping, and to return the brush to the same color when he is through. The teacher may have to help the child understand that he paints on his paper, not on his hands, his neighbor, the walls, etc. Except for these instructions, the child should be allowed to paint what he wishes without interference.

Giving a child a picture or model to copy or adding to his painting makes him dissatisfied with his works and unsure of his ability. Avoid questions and statements such as, "What did you paint? . . . Do people have purple hair? . . . Grass is green, not pink! . . . This is how to make a rabbit." Such comments show that the teacher does not value or understand the child's work. Such comments also make the child feel his work is unacceptable to the teacher. Accept a child's work as an expression of his thoughts and ideas. Encourage him with positive comments, such as "You have pretty bright colors in your picture. . . . God made our eyes so we can see (red) and (blue) colors. . . . Would you like to tell me about your painting? . . . You had fun painting today."

Children should be encouraged to clean up their work area when they are finished. Even a two year old can wipe up drips with a damp sponge or cloth.

Materials for gadget printing include paint, paper, a variety of gadgets, paper towels and shallow containers such as foil pans. Paint and paper are the same as those used for easel painting. Gadgets can come from several sources. Just use your imagination! From the kitchen use forks, cookie cutters, a potato masher, sponges, tubes from paper towels; lemons and oranges cut in half; potatoes or carrots with a design cut in the end. Use empty spools from the sewing basket. Your gadget collection might also include erasers, pipe cleaners, corks, small plastic bottles and hair rollers.

Fold two or three paper towels together to form a pad slightly smaller than the container in which they will be placed. Dampen the pad before placing it in the container. Pour paint on the pad and allow it to soak in. The child presses his gadget on the pad and then on his paper. To simplify cleaning gadgets soak them in warm, soapy water.

Gadget printing allows the child to experiment with color combinations and design. As in easel painting, the two year old should begin with one or two colors and only one or two gadgets. As his coordination improves and his experience increases, add more colors and more gadgets.

Other than giving simple directions or a demonstration of the use of the paint and gadgets, the teacher should avoid directing the activity. Resist the temptation to stop the child when YOU think his picture is "just right." The child will stop when he is satisfied that his picture is complete.

Materials for sponge painting or string painting are the same with the exception of the gadgets. For sponge painting, provide sponges cut or torn in various sizes and spring clothespins. For string painting provide lengths of string (about 8 to 12 inches long) and spring clothespins. The paper towels and saucers are not needed for string painting.

Sponge painting is similar to gadget printing; sponges are used in place of gadgets. The procedure is the same. Each sponge is held by a spring clothespin. The child uses the clothespin as a handle.

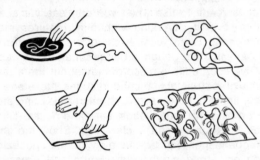

String painting is best suited for older fours and fives. Fill shallow containers with approximately one inch of paint. Clip a spring clothespin to one end of each string. The child uses the clothespin as a handle. Holding onto the clothespin, the child dips a string into the paint. He may need a paint brush to push the string into the paint. He removes the string from the paint and drags or wiggles it across his paper. He may want to plop it down and up several times. The child repeats this process until his picture is complete.

An interesting design will result if the child folds his paper in half over the string, places one hand on the paper to hold it in place and pulls the string out from between the fold.

Clay Clay and various types of salt/flour dough are excellent manipulative materials for young children. Dough can be purchased or made.[2] Potter's clay can be purchased in powdered form or already mixed and ready to use. (Do not confuse this material with the oil base modeling clay.) Powdered clay is mixed with water until it is about the consistency of bread dough. Knead the clay to distribute the moisture evenly. Let the newly made clay age until it can be handled without sticking to hands. Clay and dough must be kept in air-tight containers to prevent its drying out.

The table top should be covered when working with clay. The reverse side of oilcloth taped to a piece of heavy cardboard makes an ideal clay board. Aprons should be worn when working with clay. Sponges are needed for clean-up.

Clay is ready to use when you can easily make a thumbprint in it. (Working with clay requires more hand strength than most twos and younger threes possess; salt/flour dough is better suited to their ability.) Give each child a piece of clay about the size of a small grapefruit. As a child reaches the stage of making figures, he will break off bits of clay and stick them on as arms, legs, heads, ears and noses. These pieces will drop off as the clay dries. Show the child how appendages can be made by gently squeezing, pulling or "stroking" the clay. Fours and fives also enjoy using rolling pins and popsicle sticks to roll and cut clay.

As children work with dough or clay encourage experimentation and self-expression. Avoid providing the child with a model. Encourage the child to make an object his own way. Never allow one child to criticize another's work. "Each of us does our work the way we think is best." Give assurance and encouragement as children work. Any clay object you keep should be allowed to dry slowly away from excessive heat. These articles can be painted with tempera, shellacked or waxed.

Each child should help clean his work area and tools with a damp sponge. A dust pan and brush are needed to clean up dry crumbs of clay. Before returning the clay to its air-tight container, ask the child to roll the clay into a ball. Poke a hole in the ball and fill the hole with water. This will help keep the clay pliable. As much clay as possible should be removed from tools and hands before they are washed in the sink. Clay settles along the bottom of pipes and will clog plumbing.

Cut and Paste   For cut and paste activities, provide scissors, paper and paste. Scissors should be about four inches long with blunt points. Be sure they cut easily. Provide three or four pairs of left-handed scissors for left-handed children.

Each child should have a piece of construction paper approximately 12 inches by 18 inches on which to paste the paper he cuts. Paper for cutting can include colored construction paper, wall paper or wrapping paper. Some of the paper should be shiny and bright colored.

For five year olds, cut and paste can evolve into a tissue lamination project. Provide tissue paper in two or three different colors for this activity. A piece of manila paper can be used as a background. The child "paints" this background paper with liquid starch or diluted white glue. A wide paint brush (two or three inches wide) will do this job quickly. Next, he cuts or tears colored tissue paper into various sizes and shapes and lays them on the paper. The child completes his picture by brushing over the tissue paper with a small amount of starch or glue. Care must be taken not to get the tissue too wet. This will cause the colors to run.

Paste should be put in small containers for the child's convenience. Paper towels torn in half or pieces of waxed paper or foil, or shallow foil pans make suitable containers. When the child is finished, left-over paste can be returned to the jar and the towel thrown away.

Cut and paste is an activity probably best suited for older threes, fours, and fives. The use of scissors depends upon the development of the small hand and arm muscles. Threes and even some fours are not ready to use scissors. They will enjoy tearing the paper rather than cutting it.

Children need freedom to experiment with cut and paste activities just as they do with other art materials. At first the child seems to pile the cut pieces of paper on top of each other using big lumps of paste to stick them together. He may press the lump of paste against the paper making no attempt at smoothing it. Later he may paste the pieces he has cut so they extend over the edge of his background paper. Refrain from changing the child's work or suggesting where he paste his cut pieces.

Children should be encouraged to put paper scraps back in the box when finished. A damp sponge is needed to wipe paste off the tables and fingers. Sort through the scrap paper box periodically to remove any faded or soiled construction paper.

Collage Materials for collage can be as varied as your imagination. Include pieces of fabric, lace, paper, buttons, rickrack, string, carpeting, macaroni, straws, cotton, beads, burlap or string bags, foil, yarn, beans and peas. From outdoors gather feathers, dried weeds, seeds and seed pods, twigs, seashells, leaves, lichen, sand or gravel.

The child will need white glue or paste and a piece of heavy paper or lightweight cardboard (approximately 12 by 18 inches) on which to glue his materials. Cardboard makes a good background since some materials are too heavy for paper. Scissors will be needed to cut some of the materials.

Making a collage stimulates a child's imagination and adds to his sense of achievement. Any combination of materials can be interesting. This is an activity at which every child can succeed because there is no right or wrong way to assemble a collage. Let the child enjoy experimenting with the materials. Avoid comparing one child's work with that of another.

Place collage materials in one or two shallow boxes so a child can easily see and reach them. Making choices from too wide a selection is confusing and frustrating. It often causes him to lose interest.

Materials, such as paper and cloth, can be pasted on the background. However, objects such as buttons and twigs will require white glue. The five year old can be encouraged to arrange his materials several different ways on the background before gluing them down permanently.

Encourage good work habits by giving each child the responsibility of helping to clean up his work area.

Drawing/Coloring For coloring activities provide large sheets of paper (newsprint, butcher paper, shelf paper or the reverse side of wallpaper or wrapping paper) and large crayons. The paper should be no smaller than 12" by 18".

Large or jumbo crayons about four inches long and 3/8 inch in diameter, are easily held by young children. Some crayons should have the paper removed so the child can use the sides of the crayon. Periodically sort out and discard short, unusable crayons.

Five year olds may enjoy combining a coloring activity with finger painting. These children will need aprons, liquid paint, in addition to paper and crayons. To finger-paint over a crayon design the child must color very heavily on the sheet of paper. Next, he finger-paints over the crayon design. He will need to dig down through the paint so parts of the crayoning will show through the design in his finger painting. Or, he can smooth the paint evenly over his paper and use a popsicle stick to scrape through to the crayoning.

Coloring or drawing is the one art activity with which most young children have had some experience at home. Provide materials and let the child draw and color in the way he thinks best. (Of course, limits are necessary. No child should be allowed to color table, toys, walls or himself!) Show enthusiasm and interest in the child's work. Avoid passing judgment or asking "What is it?" Praise his efforts. "Tommy, you are working very hard on your picture. . . . Janie, I like the bright colors in your picture."

The young child is capable of expressing himself

through his own marks or pictures. He does not need outlines such as found in coloring books. These predetermined shapes help undermine his creative development and his self-confidence. They tend to make him feel dissatisfied with his own efforts. The young child's small muscle development does not allow him to color within the lines as expected in coloring books.

BIBLE TEACHING/LEARNING OPPORTUNITIES

All art activities lend themselves to the Bible teaching/learning aims of SHARING, KINDNESS and HELPING. It is usually necessary for the children to share materials and wait turns. Every child should be responsible for helping to clean his own work area. As children work identify specific acts of acceptable behavior. Use the following ideas and Bible Thoughts in your conversation: "Stacey is sharing her sponge with Mark. Our Bible tells us to *share with others*. . . . You are a kind helper, Brad. Thank you for picking up those spilled crayons. . . . Thank you for clipping Cheryl's paper on the easel, Greg. Our Bible tells us to *help each other* . . . Jack may put the brushes in the water to soak. Mary may throw the newspapers away. Craig may put the paint on the sink. When we help each other we clean up very quickly."

Bible Thoughts for your conversation:

Help each other. Proverbs 12:12 *(The Living Bible)*

Treat others with kindness. Galatians 6:10

Be . . . kind to one another. Ephesians 4:32

CREATION

As the children work, use these Bible Thoughts and ideas in your conversation:

"You have a seed pod on your collage, Betsy. God planned for seeds to grow in seed pods. The seeds blew away. Now the pod is empty. It's what you need for your collage. . . . God made your hands just right for finger painting, Charles. *It is God who has made us*. . . . Clay is a special kind of dirt. God made the dirt. *All things were made by God*."

Bible Thoughts for your conversation:
God . . . made the world and everything in it.
Acts 17:24

There is nothing too hard for [God]. Jeremiah 32:17

All things were made by [God]. John 1:3

[God] . . . made everything. Ecclesiastes 3:11

It is God who has made us. Psalm 100:3

THANKFULNESS

The young child can learn to be thankful for hands with which to work and eyes with which to see colors, shapes and designs. He can be thankful for his materials and for friends with whom he has happy times. To respond in thankfulness, a child needs an adult to help him be aware of God's loving care. "I'm glad God made our hands just right for holding a paint brush. We can tell God 'thank you' for our hands. . . . What color is the button you put on your collage, John? How did you know? We can tell God 'thank you' for eyes to see colors . . . We had fun using clay today. Let's tell God 'thank you' for clay. *It is good to give thanks to the Lord.*" A child's smile as well as other expressions of joy are also a part of his response of thankfulness.

Bible Thoughts for your conversation:
I thank God. 2 Timothy 1:3

O Give thanks to the Lord; for He is good. Psalm 136:1

It is good . . . to give thanks to the Lord. Psalm 92:1

Be thankful [to God]. Psalm 100:4

STOP! *Before you continue:*

☐ *Note the Bible teaching / learning aim for the next unit you will be teaching. Select an art activity new to your children and appropriate to the aim to use during that unit. Jot down appropriate Bible verses and conversation to relate the activity to the aim.*

☐ *Plan now to collect material for collage and gadgets for gadget printing. List some of the materials or gadgets you already have to start your collection.*

FOOTNOTES

PART III

INTRODUCTION
1. James 1:22
2. John 1:3
3. Ephesians 6:1
4. Hebrews 13:16

CHAPTER 9
1. Haystead, *Ways to Plan and Organize*

CHAPTER 10
1. John 1:3
2. Haystead, *Ways to Plan and Organize*

CHAPTER 11
1. Haystead, *Ways to Plan and Organize*
2. Doan, Eleanor, *Equipment Encyclopedia,* (Glendale, Calif.: G/L Publications, 1962).

CHAPTER 12
1. Self, Margaret M. *202 Things to Do,* (Glendale, Calif.: Regal Books, 1968).
2. Matthew 14:14-21; Mark 6:30-44; Luke 9:10-17; John 4:1-14
3. John 4:3-42
4. Mark 4:35-41; Matthew 8:23-27; Luke 8:22-25
5. Genesis 28:10-22
6. *Little Ones Sing,* Revised Edition, (Glendale, Calif.: G/L Publications, 1972).
7. *More Sing-a-Long Songs for Little Ones,* LP record with accompaniment and narration, (Glendale, Calif.: G/L Publications).
8. Doan, Eleanor, *Equipment Encyclopedia, (Glendale, Calif: G/L Publications, 1962).*

CHAPTER 13
1. Haystead, *Ways to Plan and Organize*
2.. Self, Margaret M. *158 Things to Make,* (Glendale, Calif.: G/L Publications, 1969).

BIBLIOGRAPHY

Baker, Katherine R. and Fane, Xenia F. *Understanding and Guiding Young Children.* Englewood Cliffs, N.J.: Prentice-Hall, 1967.

Chandler, E. Bessie. *Early Learning Experiences.* Van Nuys, Calif.: Instructors Publications, 1970.

Fritz, Dorothy B. *The Child and the Christian Faith.* Chicago: The Covenant Press, 1964.

Fritz, Dorothy B. *The Spiritual Growth of Children.* Philadelphia: Westminster Press.

Gale, Elizabeth Wright. *Have You Tried This?* Valley Forge, Pa.: The Judson Press, 1960.

Gilliland, Anne Hitchcock. *Understanding Preschoolers.* Nashville: Convention Press, 1969.

Gospel Light Publications. *Loan-of-a-Life Kit #1, #2.* Glendale, Calif.: G/L Publications, 1967.

Hearn, Florence Conner. *Guiding Preschoolers.* Nashville: Convention Press, 1969.

Hollander, H. Cornelia. *Portable Workshop for Pre-School Teachers.* New York: Doubleday & Company, Inc., 1966.

Hymes, James, Jr. *A Child Development Point of View.* Englewood Cliffs, N.J.: Prentice-Hall, 1955.

Leeper, S. H. *Good School for Young Children.* The Macmillan Company: New York, 1969.

Leach, Joan and Elliott, Patricia, *First Steps.* Cincinnati: Standard Publishing Company, 1965.

Newbury, Josephine. *Church Kindergarten Resource Book.* Chicago: The Covenant Press, 1964.

Nicholson, Dorothy. *Toward Effective Teaching.* Anderson, Ind.: Warner Press, Inc., 1970

Pitcher, Lasher, Feinburg and Hammond. *Helping Young Children Learn.* Columbus, Ohio: Charles E. Merrill Publishing Company, 1966.

Read, Katherine H. *Nursery School:* A Human Relationships Laboratory. Philadelphia: W. B. Saunders Company, 1966.

Sibley, Leonard A. *Help, A Guide for New Church School Teachers.* Philadelphia: Lutheran Church Press, 1967.

U.S. Department of Health, Education, Welfare. *Your Child From 1 to 6.* Washington, D.C.: U.S. Government Printing Office, 1962.

Woodard, Carol. *Ways to Teach 3's to 5's.* Philadelphia: Lutheran Church Press, 1965.

Wylie, Joanne, ed. *A Creative Guide for Preschool Teachers.* Racine, Wisc.: Western Publishing Education, 1965.

Young, Lois Horton. *Teaching Kindergarten Children.* Valley Forge, Pa.: Judson Press, 1959.

Zimmerman, Eleanor. *Bible and Doctrine for 3's to 5's.* Philadelphia: Lutheran Church Press, 1963.

LEAFLETS AND MAGAZINES

Childhood Education Magazine. Association for Childhood Education, International.

Creating with Materials for Work and Play. Association for Childhood Education, International.

Interaction Magazine. Allan Hart Jahsmann, editor, Concordia Publishing House, February, 1970.

Kindergarten Portfolio. Association for Childhood Education, International, 1969-70.

Learning Experiences for Young Children. National Council of the Churches of Christ in the USA.

Nursery School Portfolio. Association for Childhood Education, International.

Young Children Magazine. National Association for the Education of Young Children.

While each of these books is considered helpful, the publisher does not necessarily endorse the complete contents.